FOR THIS CAUSE

FOR THIS CAUSE

FINDING THE MEANING OF LIFE,
AND LIVING A LIFE OF MEANING

BRIAN HOUSTON

PUBLISHED BY MAXIMISED LEADERSHIP INC.

FOR THIS CAUSE
First published July 2001
Second impression October 2001
Third impression February 2002

Copyright © 2001 Brian Houston

Scripture quotations are taken from the New King James Version.
Copyright © 1982 by Thomas Nelson, Inc. Used by permission. All rights
reserved.

Bold or italicised emphasis in scriptures is author's own.

All song lyrics quoted are taken from 'For This Cause' ©2000 Hillsong
Publishing. All songs used by permission.

National Library of Australia:
Cataloguing-in-Publication data:

      Houston, Brian.
      For this cause : finding the meaning of life, and living a
      life of meaning.

      ISBN 0 9577336 5 8.

      1. Spiritual life - Christianity. 2. Self-actualization (Psychology) -
      Religious aspects - Christianity. 3. Philosophy. 4. Life. I. Title.

      248.25

Cover design by Richard Pritchard, Sydney Media Collective,
www.sydneymediacollective.com.au

Back cover photograph by Femia Shirtliff.

Printed by J S McMillan Printing, Lidcombe, NSW, Australia

Published by Maximised Leadership Incorporated,
PO Box 1195, Castle Hill, NSW 1765 Australia
www.maximisedleadership.com

DEDICATION

To all those past and present
who have made the choice to
live for the Cause of Jesus Christ, and
put the Kingdom first in everything they do.

CONTENTS

INTRODUCTION

THE CAUSE

One Sunday evening in March 2000, our church united to praise and glorify God in one accord. They came from all over Sydney, bringing together the congregations of the City and Hills worship centres, as well as those of our many outreach services.

What a sight to see – thousands of people, young and old, filling the Homebush State Sports Centre to capacity. Nearly six months later, this same venue would draw crowds to watch world-class athletes compete in the 2000 Olympic Games, but that night the acclamation, adoration and applause was for one person – Jesus Christ. Truly the presence of God was awesome in that place, and there was only one reason for such love, joy, unity and commitment: The Cause of Christ!

The result of that Sunday night church service was the live recording of *For This Cause*, our first praise and worship album for the new millennium. The

Cause of the King and the Kingdom is the basis of everything we do. It is the reason why the songs on the Hillsong albums are written, and it is the reason why the songs on these albums are sung in churches all over the world. It is the reason why I preach and teach the Word of God, and it is the reason why I am writing this book.

This book is all about the power of a cause. Having a sense of purpose, with a specific aim and direction, gives meaning and power to life. Sadly, so many people settle for a bland, empty existence, and never discover the real reason for their lives. But the Cause changes all that.

FINDING YOUR REASON FOR LIVING

You may recall a popular song written a few decades ago that laments an ended love affair. The lyrics of the chorus say, "There goes my reason for living ... there goes my everything."

What could make *you* feel so empty and hopeless inside that you lose your reason for living? Would it be a person, a job or career, an ideology or philosophy that could cause a loss of purpose or direction? Perhaps you have yet to establish your reason for living? Some people live to make money, but possessions or success won't bring deep fulfillment to the emptiness in people's lives. There are many unhappy people walking about in Armani suits, and driving luxury cars.

In the midst of our society, where there is so much superficiality, cynicism and skepticism, I know people are searching for answers and looking for something to believe in. Within every one of us is a desire for purpose, and a longing for significance, acceptance and unconditional love.

At some stage, every human being will contemplate the 'meaning of life.' The truth is that if you don't discover the meaning of life, you will never live a life of meaning. When you get a revelation of the Cause, your life will certainly have meaning.

My hope is that this book will inspire you to find the answers to three significant questions:

1. Have you discovered the reason why you were **born**?

2. Have you determined your motivation for **living**? and

3. Have you decided what you would be prepared to **die** for?

FOR THIS CAUSE

PART I

BORN
FOR THE CAUSE

CHAPTER ONE

FOR THIS CAUSE
I WAS BORN

'FOR THIS CAUSE
I WAS BORN,
AND FOR THIS CAUSE
I HAVE COME
INTO THE WORLD'

– Jesus Christ

[John 18:37]

CHAPTER 1

FOR THIS CAUSE
I WAS BORN

An innocent man stood in front of a judge, facing a barrage of questions that would ultimately determine his future. This was to be one of the greatest trials in recorded history, but he didn't have a vast legal team of attorneys or lawyers advising him what to say or how to plead. He answered the questions directed at him with dignity and conviction, declaring a truth so absolute that it confounded those present.

The governor of the state then asked a probing question: "Are you a king then?" He received a powerful, definitive answer:

"For you say rightly that I am a King. *For this cause* I was born, and *for this cause* I have come into the world." [John 18:37]

'For this cause' – it is a statement of certainty and conviction. Jesus Christ knew who He was, and what the purpose of His life was. He also knew why He would die. He had spoken of His death, declaring "but for this cause, I came to this hour" (John 12: 27). His entire life was encapsulated in that one powerful phrase – '*for this cause.*'

I love His boldness and certainty. He carried no doubt and He knew the answers to the significant questions that every human being also asks: why He was born, why He was on earth, and why He would die. These are the same three questions the Cause will answer in your life.

In my life, I am committed to the Cause of Christ. The Cause is what I live for, and it affects my behaviour, my thinking and my motivation. I don't wake up every morning and wonder what I should do with my life. Deep down I know I was born for His Cause, and nothing can change that.

In my first book, *Get A Life*, I wrote about colliding with life and discovering destiny. Your life is not a result of powerless fate, but is attached to a pre-determined purpose that originated in the mind of God. He has an awesome plan and purpose for your life that goes well beyond you. You were born for the Cause of the King and the Kingdom.

Jesus Himself taught us to seek first the Kingdom, but what, you may ask, is the Kingdom of God? The Kingdom is not a mystical place up in the clouds, but includes everything in the realm of Christ. Having Kingdom purpose involves bringing the abundance of heaven to earth, and a revelation of that fact will change your life.

There are those who look at their life in hopeless despair and say "I wish I'd never been born." Without the Cause, the futility of life can be frustrating and will prevent you from seeing your connection to the world – relationships, talents, anointing and calling will have no purpose. But when you get a revelation of the Cause, suddenly everything has purpose and meaning. When you stand firmly on the Word of God, you also begin to see a much bigger picture as the Cause puts everything into perspective.

And suddenly you find that life makes sense and *you* can also state with conviction: "For this Cause, I was born!"

CHAPTER TWO

YOU ARE NOT HERE
BY ACCIDENT

'WHAT TO SAY, LORD? ... IT'S YOU WHO GAVE ME LIFE'

CHAPTER 2

YOU ARE NOT HERE BY ACCIDENT

C hristine Caine is a dynamic leader in our church whose unwavering passion and zeal to see people switched on to the Cause of Christ is her life's call. Her ministry has involved raising and training youth leadership, and today she is a popular communicator who travels extensively around Australia and the globe.

But go back some twelve years, and you would have encountered an angry young woman in her early twenties, wrestling with issues that stemmed from a strict Greek Orthodox heritage, abuse and a sense of inferiority because of her socio-economic background. Giving her life to Jesus Christ gave her the sense of direction and purpose that comes with knowing you have an awesome God-given destiny to fulfil. Christine became actively involved in our church youth group, and her life started on the course that has enabled her to go and do what she once could have only imagined.

Yet her story doesn't end there. Prior to her thirty-third birthday, Christine discovered she had been adopted at birth. This startling news came as a huge shock, and it could easily have thrown her off course and caused her to question her identity. But she never wavered from her sense of destiny and purpose. Regardless of the circumstances of her birth, she knew she was alive for the Cause of the King and the Kingdom. Nothing could ever change that.

I don't know what the circumstances of your birth or upbringing were, but they do not change one very potent truth: you were also born for a cause ... the Cause of the King and the Kingdom.

JESUS HIMSELF HAD EVERY REASON NOT TO SUCCEED

Consider the less-than-ideal circumstances surrounding the birth of Jesus. In today's society, He would almost certainly be classified as one from a dysfunctional background. He had every reason to grow up to be the one most-likely-*not*-to-succeed.

First of all, He was born to a young teenage girl, who at the time of conception wasn't even married. Secondly, the man she married, Joseph, wasn't actually His biological father. Thirdly, His *real* father was an unusual entity. Imagine Jesus as a young boy in the school playground as other boys boasted about their dads. How difficult would it have been explaining to His friends that His father was actually God in heaven?

There are many other circumstances surrounding His actual birth that were also rather abnormal. His mother was whisked off to another town for His birth, and He was instantly pursued by a paranoid king. He certainly wasn't born in a sterilised hospital delivery room, surrounded with the comforts of life. We often create images of cosy nativity scenes on Christmas cards, but the reality is that of a stable with rats, vermin, and a lingering stench.

From early childhood, He was faced with the enormous pressure of expectation. The scriptures declared that "the government shall be upon His shoulders" (see Isaiah 9:6) so Jesus had a lot to live up to.

The Bible also says that when Jesus was born the angels sang, "Peace on earth, goodwill to *all* men." But not 'all men' responded gladly to Him. He was despised, mocked and condemned to death. Jesus had to deal with the pain of rejection, yet that didn't hold Him back. Every one of us have experienced some degree of rejection in life, but if you allow it to leave its mark on your life, it will. People who harbour insecurity and rejection usually push others away, sabotaging the very things they long for, such as love and acceptance.

There are others who may be ruled by the experience of betrayal or broken trust. Jesus was betrayed by one in His closest circle of friends. In His home town of Nazareth, He was given no respect or honour, and the Word tells us that He was therefore unable to perform any miracles there.

Another thing Jesus faced wherever He went was continual persecution from the Pharisees. Such a bombardment of religious legalism would have probably caused most of us to feel bogged down and persecuted, yet He rose above every challenge and obstacle.

On human terms, Jesus Christ had plenty of reasons to fail in life, but 2000 years on, His birth, His life and His death continues to influence and impact the world. It wasn't the circumstances of His birth, or the opinions of people that determined His purpose or direction. He didn't live out His life from a position of insecurity, negativity or rejection, because He knew He was on earth for the Cause. That sense of Cause put *everything* in perspective.

Once you understand the power of the Cause, everything else falls into place, and that is when you can start becoming all that God has called you to be. Instead of being ruled by the circumstances of your birth or the limitations of your background, you can move forward into God's plan.

REBEL WITHOUT A CAUSE

In the 1950s, the young actor James Dean soared to stardom in the movie *Rebel Without a Cause*. Based on an actual case study of a delinquent youth with psychopathic tendencies, this film achieved cult status, glamourising the rebellious youth of that era. The tragedy is that the very incidents reflected in the movie are typical issues and conflicts that face so many young people today. 'Without a cause' is such an apt definition of a rebel.

I love seeing young people sold out for the Cause of Christ. They still have the same issues to face and are searching for answers to their many questions, but the difference is that life within this Cause provides purpose, meaning, and answers.

Many are unable to discover their purpose in life because their perspective is clouded by so many issues. Someone who has allowed rejection or offence to direct their life will see everything from that position. Jesus faced constant criticism and rejection, and He could have easily felt hurt and offended, yet He didn't allow those things to stop Him from fulfilling His purpose.

As a young man at Bible College, I was taught that no matter what occurred in life, never allow yourself to develop a 'wounded spirit.' That wisdom has stuck with me ever since. As a result, I have never looked at my life in terms of what I lacked or what happened to me, but according to the knowledge that I was born for the Cause of the King and the Kingdom. It has equipped me to confront and rise above inadequacies, lack and feelings that may have limited or contained me. Even in my forties I have been confronted by some extraordinary twists in life, but I know my foundation – Jesus!

Some people never get over the circumstances of their birth or upbringing, and it prevents them from moving forward in life. There may be certain things that happened in your past, but the power of those negative situations can be broken so that they don't affect you today. Instead of being ruled by the circumstances, allow the reality that you were born for an awesome reason to penetrate your heart. If you can look at your life from the position of the Cause of the King and the Kingdom, what you see will dramatically change.

So why are you on earth today? It wasn't the luck of the draw. Think about this: you are a one-in-a-million success story from the moment of your conception. There is no mistake about who you are, and who you are destined to be. Look at what God says about you:

"Before I formed you in the womb I knew you; before you were born I sanctified you." [Jeremiah 1:5]

David also had a revelation of God's hand on his life, declaring:

"For You formed my inward parts; You covered me in my mother's womb." [Psalm 139: 13]

When you get a revelation of the Cause, no matter what comes against you in life, it won't be able to throw you off course. Discouragement, depression or the frustrations of life won't be able to pull you down. Knowing that you were born for a Cause will keep you moving forward and release you into the plans and purposes of God.

CHAPTER THREE

VISION FUELLED BY A CAUSE

'LET ALL I AM BE
ALL YOU WANT ME TO BE'

– Lyrics from '*For This Cause*'
[©2000 Joel Houston/Hillsong Publishing]

CHAPTER 3

VISION FUELLED BY A CAUSE

I clearly remember two young men who each had specific dreams and goals for their future. On separate occasions, they each shared their personal vision for their lives with me. Both of them had outstanding business acumen, with the potential of great success in the corporate world.

The first one confidently told me his vision. "Brian, my ambition is to be a millionnaire by the age of 30!" He had set himself a goal and he certainly had the determination and potential to achieve it.

But the vision of the second young man impressed me more. "Brian," he said, "my personal vision is to fund and finance the salvation of the earth." What a powerful perspective he placed on his gift and talent. To him, money was a tool which could do great things for the Cause of the King and the Kingdom.

It is great to have goals and ambitions in life, but the second man's vision is more powerful because it is linked to a cause. A vision without a cause is little more than a set of personal goals. A vision attached to a cause is more than a hit-and-miss affair – that vision has *power*!

A lot has been spoken and written about vision in recent years, and there is no doubt that having a specific vision gives one direction and purpose. I love hanging around great visionaries because they challenge and inspire me. It is rather like iron sharpening iron, stirring up creativity and innovative ideas.

The Word of God speaks about vision, and how people live carelessly without it. It also tells us to write the vision and make it plain so that he may run who reads it (see Habbakuk 2:2). When a group of people get behind a vision – be it the vision of a church, a movement, or a business enterprise – that vision adds impetus and life to that organisation. I believe that a vision or a set of goals keeps us focused and gives us direction.

WHAT IS MORE IMPORTANT: A VISION OR A CAUSE?

While it is essential to have vision and to be people of vision, a cause is much more powerful. We talk a lot about vision, destiny and dreams, but it is on the foundation of a cause that vision is birthed. One translation of Proverbs 29:18 says that "where there is no *progressive revelation*, the people perish or die." A continual unfolding revelation of the Cause of Christ will empower any vision and give it purpose. Vision is so much more powerful when it serves a cause.

The same principle of cause and effect comes into operation with a vision and a cause. When you direct your motivation, thinking, talent, or relationships towards the Cause, you will have a greater effect. When you are committed to a cause, you don't have to make up a vision because that cause is the foundation or basis out of which vision flows. Vision is essential, but the Cause is powerful.

A vision can be personal, but a cause is bigger than any one person

People can talk about their vision with excitement and enthusiasm that motivates others, but the reality is that a cause is greater than any one individual or person. I have my personal vision, and our church has its own vision statement, but the Cause of Christ is bigger than one church.

Naturally I am delighted when people understand and catch the vision of our church, but I am aware that it is far more powerful when people get switched on to the Cause of Christ. It is the Cause that will impact and change their lives forever. If our church has the Cause in their spirit, they will automatically partner in our corporate vision, and will live lives overflowing with personal vision.

All the denominations and ministries throughout the world that exalt Jesus Christ exist for the Cause of the King and the Kingdom. I love the diversity within the landscape of the Church, because there is room for different vision and mission statements, but the Cause embraces them all. This is because the Cause is so much bigger than any one of us.

A vision is something you possess, but a cause possesses you

Jesus was captivated and consumed by the Cause. It affected and directed every aspect of His life. It wasn't something He possessed, but the Cause possessed Him.

When you are committed to a cause, you don't have to make up a vision for your life. It takes hold of you and begins to influence everything you do.

You wouldn't die for a vision, but you will die for a cause

In the days following the demise of the Soviet Union, the attention of the world media was drawn to the little town of Grozny, where a small group of Chechneyan rebels made a stand against the might of the Russian army. They weren't fighting for a vision, they were fighting to the death for their cause. Similarly, suicide bombers have chosen to give their lives for the sake of their cause. People won't die for someone else's vision, but many choose to die for a cause, no matter how violent or misguided it can be. You may have a fantastic vision for your life, and there may be those who get excited about it, but there won't be many who will die for it.

Jesus predicted His death on the cross, saying, "But for this cause, I come to this hour" (John 12:27). He never died for a vision, but He willingly gave His life for the Cause. As a church leader, I know that the Cause is far more powerful in the hearts of a congregation than commitment to a vision. It amazes me how willingly those who have a revelation of the King and the Kingdom will lay down their lives for the sake of the Cause.

A vision has options, but
a cause leaves you with no choice

When Jesus told His disciples about His death, He knew there was no other way:

"Now my soul is troubled and what shall I say? Father, save me from this hour." [John 12:27]

A vision has options. If things become discouraging, you can put it aside or you can change direction. You can choose to run with a vision, or you can choose to abandon it. You hold a vision in your hand, but a cause holds you in its hand. The Apostle Paul spoke about how the love of God compelled him. In other words it left him with no other choice. When your life is gripped by a cause, the options disappear.

As a pastor of a church, I don't have a 'normal' weekend the way other people do. Hillsong Church has a city-wide network of cell groups, two major worship centres and (at the time of writing this) 15 outreach services around Sydney which are all part of the one entity. Our two worship centres are separated by a 35 minute drive and currently share six Friday night youth meetings, and ten weekend church services. Obviously, the leisure of reading the Sunday newspapers over a cappuccino at a beachside café, or the smell of a freshly mown lawn is not a part of my usual Sunday routine, but I never feel like I'm missing out, because I'm doing what I was born to do. As a teenager I realised that to pursue God's call on my life would mean that Sundays would never be my own. Above anything else, I love serving God and ministering the Word. It is the Cause of Christ that compels me.

A vision can be ignored, but
you cannot ignore a cause

At some stage, you may have had a Schweppes soft drink to quench your thirst. You probably didn't give much thought to the vision of the company. When Bobbie and I were first married, I worked as a sales rep for Schweppes in Auckland, and at the same time I volunteered as the youth leader in my local church. When I started, they gave me a huge manual which contained information about the company, its founder, and its mission statement. I was expected to read it and know their vision. I gave my best in the year I worked there (and I appreciated the company car and salary) but I must confess that I already had a vision for my life, and that involved the Cause of Christ.

You may drive through a city and pass many large corporations and businesses. It is likely that most of them will have a mission statement. You may recognise their name or their logo, but it is unlikely you would take long to consider what their vision is.

The point is that you can ignore someone else's vision, but *you cannot ignore a cause*. No matter what you think about the IRA (Irish Republican Army) you cannot pretend they don't exist, especially if you live in Belfast. The fact is that they are motivated by a cause and cannot be ignored. If the Cause of Christ takes hold of your life or your church, those around you will not be able to ignore it either.

CHAPTER FOUR

EMPOWERING THE VISION

'THAT YOU WOULD GUIDE ME IN EVERY SINGLE STEP I TAKE'

CHAPTER 4

EMPOWERING YOUR VISION

Mathematics was never my forté. During my school years in New Zealand, I received 18 per cent for school certificate mathematics. Yet when I went to Bible College, I got 99 percent in the first exam I sat. The difference between my attitude at school and to Bible College related directly to motivation. With hindsight I can see that I was unwise, but I found school very demotivating. However, after making a conscious choice to spend my life serving God at the age of 17, my life became consumed with 'the Cause,' and I was motivated by new vision.

That life's vision has been fuelled and empowered by my commitment to the Cause of Christ. My own determination and ability could only have taken me so far, and it has been the grace and favour of God that has resulted in me pastoring a church that is having great impact and influence today. When people ask about the success of Hillsong music, we cannot attribute it to a vision or a goal. The songs that are written by our worship team serve the Cause of the King and the Kingdom.

A vision will generate excitement, but a cause generates power

I receive many invitations to speak at churches and conferences all over the world, but I remember one invitation that stood out, even though I was unable to accept. It was a request to minister in India and what touched me was the vision statement of that ministry. Their aim was to give every Indian citizen one fair chance to hear the Gospel. Now that is a powerful vision, because the power behind it is the Cause.

The Apostle Paul wrote:

"I am not ashamed of the Gospel of Christ because it is the **power** of God unto salvation." [Romans 1:16]

Vision generates excitement and enthusiasm, but the Cause *generates power*. If you allow the Cause to penetrate your life, it will *empower* your relationships, your plans for the future and your connection to the world.

A vision can exist for you, but you exist for the Cause

One of the differences between having a vision and living for a cause is that a vision can exist for your own purposes and interests. When it comes to a cause, you exist for the sake of it.

It is easy to develop the thinking that 'the Church exists for me.' During one of my ministry trips, the youth leader of a church fetched me from the airport. I asked him about his work and he began to tell me how frustrated he was because the pastor of the church wouldn't get behind his vision. My reply to him was, "It isn't your pastor's job to get behind your vision. It is your job to work out what his vision is, and get behind that." His mistake was in thinking that his church existed for him and his vision, when in fact he existed to fulfil the Cause, and serve it through the vision of his church.

When you get too many visions, you actually end up getting di-vision. In our church, we don't have one vision for the women's ministry, another vision for the youth, or a separate vision for the creative team. We have one vision for the church, and that is outworked through all the various departments (women, youth, music, creative, technical, children, television, etc). Yet even within our vision, we exist for the Cause. Once people have a sense of the Cause, it is amazing how much enthusiasm and commitment is injected into the ministry. The Message Bible says it this way:

> "Each part (of the body) gets its meaning from the body as a whole, not the other way around." [Romans 12:4]

When the purpose of your vision is not so much about you, but is for the sake of something much bigger, you discover the *power* of the Cause. This involves living a life well beyond yourself. Those who are sick don't merely receive their healing for themselves, but so that they can be effective for the Kingdom. Business people who prosper financially aren't blessed so that they can store up wealth for themselves – their resource enables them to help others in a far greater capacity than had they not prospered.

Only the best of visions will outlast you, but a cause is eternal

One of the highest rewards I receive is when someone tells me how a message that I once taught changed their life, or a book I have written has transformed their thinking. That isn't about my vision, it's about His Cause which has such eternal value in that it impacts the lives of others.

I have a big vision for our church. Many years ago when we held our church services in a rented warehouse, I dreamed of the day we would own land and build a great building. Well, we have recently commenced the next phase of that building project.

Yet the reality is that one day a new generation will take over my vision and run with their own vision (which will hopefully be bigger and better than mine!) The young people of today have increased skills and strengths, and I pray that my vision will be too small for them. Buildings and land may outlast me and my vision, but the Cause of the King and the Kingdom will continue into eternity.

A vision is allowed to change, but the Cause never changes

There are times when we need to modify our vision or perhaps even change or expand it. I know that my vision has evolved and grown over the years. You can change your vision any time you choose to, but it would be unwise to change it too often. I'd give our church motion sickness if I kept changing direction all the time.

I find one of the most challenging church services of the year to prepare for is our Vision Sunday which is when we inspire the church for the new year ahead. The reality is that our vision hasn't changed that much since we started the church – all we are doing today is outworking the same vision we began with in a little school hall in 1983.

There are those who always try and come up with new vision to generate more excitement, but the key is to *build* on the vision God has already given you. A vision can certainly evolve and grow, but the Cause itself never changes. When I was 29, I didn't realise how much our vision would encompass in later years. As we have progressed and increased, our vision has needed to embrace the expansion and growth.

When Bobbie and I took over the leadership of my father's church in 1999, it was a tremendous honour. Our own church in the Hills was birthed out of the original vision of that City church, yet since every church ultimately reflects the vision and heartbeat of its pastor or leader, over the years I had developed my own vision. Many people in the City church were committed to the vision they had been pursuing for many years (and so they ought to have been, because it was a great vision). Yet if the City church had been built on vision alone, there could have been absolute turmoil, division and confusion, because we have constantly added change and transition to unify the vision of both congregations. But what kept the City church together was the Cause.

As we began to unite as **one church** with two worship centres and two teams of staff members (but with a single vision and administration), we began to see them miraculously come together with ease and harmony. While the vision had changed, the Cause within their hearts remained the same.

Our church has remained solid and has continued to grow because it is built on more than vision – it is built around the Cause. Today as the Hillsong Church, we operate as one, outworking our vision for the Cause of the King and the Kingdom through our two major worship centres, the city-wide network of cell groups, and the many contributing services and ministries.

If people are linked together because of the Cause, even when there is a shift in vision, they will continue to move forward. It is not just about us or our vision, but about the Cause which is eternal and never changes.

When you get behind His Cause,
He will get behind your vision

By surrendering your life to His Cause, He will breathe life into your vision. Jesus said that if anyone left houses, land or families for the sake of the Gospel [the Cause] they would receive a one hundredfold return (see Mark 10:29,30).

When your focus is on the Cause, you will experience the blessing of God. On its own, a vision has limitations, but when linked to the Cause of Christ, it has supernatural power and purpose. Any vision is only as powerful as the cause that it is linked to.

CHAPTER FIVE
CAUSE AND EFFECT

'MORE THAN I COULD
HOPE AND DREAM OF
YOU HAVE POURED
YOUR FAVOUR ON ME'

CHAPTER 5

CAUSE AND EFFECT

E very cause will have an effect, just as every symptom has a source. So the effect of the Cause in your life will have a particular outcome – the blessing of God.

Throughout the Bible, you can read the countless promises of God to His people. Surprisingly, there are those who read the Word and only see the warnings, or "thou shalt nots." Others see the promises of blessing, and ignore the conditions. You cannot have Bible results if you don't live according to Bible principles, in the same way that what you sow you will reap. When you live according to the Cause, it will have a life-changing effect!

Looking at it this way, when someone gets their eyes off the Cause, it weakens the effect. Going to church in itself won't change anything, and being a Christian will not guarantee a great marriage. The power of having a cause in your life is that it is *persuasive*. It establishes your convictions, determines your priorities and sets your standards. Even Pontius Pilate was persuaded that Jesus was innocent. He said he could find no fault with Him.

A cause is also emotive. No-one can be impartial about Jesus Christ, and the mention of His name will always stir up some kind of emotion. The same crowd who had given Him a tremendous welcome into Jerusalem the week before, called for His crucifixion and cried for the release of Barabbas a week later. In the same way, the message of the Gospel stirs up people's emotions today.

There are those who profess to love God and honour Jesus Christ as His Son, but they claim to dislike the Church. It always saddens me because Jesus loves His Church – He calls it His body and His bride. In fact, He declared, "I will build My Church and the gates of hell will not prevail against it." Throughout the earth the Church is the vehicle through which He draws people to Himself, building broken lives and commissioning them to reach others. Freely we have received, so freely we should give.

PURSUING THE CAUSE OF THE CHURCH

When you pursue the Cause of the King and the Kingdom in a dynamic local church, the scientific law of cause and effect comes into operation. When you lay down self to serve His Cause, there will be an effect!

The Word promises that those planted in the house of the Lord will flourish (see Psalm 92:13,14). You can expect your life to increase and prosper if you plant yourself in God's house, and here are seven things that you can expect to happen in your life.

1. You will enlarge and expand

Gideon was amazed that God wanted to use him as a deliverer of Israel, because he saw himself as inferior and small. However, God knew his potential and saw him as a mighty man of valour. The result was that he was stretched, enlarged and became an awesome man of God.

Pursuing the Cause in a dynamic local church has the capacity to remove any negative, defeated thinking you may have about yourself. Those things that held you back or hurt you won't be as important as serving the King and the Kingdom. The Cause is always bigger than any one individual, and as you embrace it, you will expand and increase in your capacity. A commitment to *His* world will dramatically increase *your* world.

2. You will maximise your gift

There was a businessman in our church who started his own enterprise but over time, he began to lose interest in it. It became smaller and less productive until it finally died. He was in church one day when he got a revelation that his gift for business could have Kingdom purpose. Consequently his vision for business stirred up again, but this time his company was fashioned with a specific purpose and a reason to succeed. From that point, his business was fuelled with new energy as it was built around the Cause of the King and the Kingdom.

The Apostle Paul urges us to stir up the gift within us (2 Timothy 1: 6). A church that is vibrant and alive will stir up gifts, and become an outlet or vehicle for those gifts and talents to be outworked. Gifted people who have no vehicle long to be discovered, and when they sow their gift into the church where they are planted, not only do they help *build* that church but their gift finds an *outlet*.

3. You will develop leadership skills

When a church operates and functions successfully, it is usually because of good leadership. I certainly never learned any leadership qualities in school. I was never voted school captain or elected to a school council, but any leadership skills I do have were honed in the church.

The Church has produced some outstanding leaders over time. Youth ministry is an excellent nursery for up-and-coming leaders, and I've seen many young people blossom, increase and develop into great leaders, both in church life and in their careers.

I believe every believer is called to be a leader in that others should see and follow their example. It is those who are passionately commited to the Cause who will have a significant impact in effectively influencing the lives of others.

4. You will build relationships

How sad when a single girl believes she has to hang out in a pub to meet a man, or when a young man relies on Internet chat rooms to find friends. The longing for a meaningful relationship drives people to resort to such desperate measures.

I'm not suggesting anyone attend church only to meet people, but when you come for the right reasons, you will inevitably build various levels of relationships into your life that will bless you. If your life is committed to the Cause, then where else but His Church will you find a better partner with a kindred commitment?

5. You will strengthen in character

As you build your life according to the Word of God, you begin to build character. Paul wrote to Titus about revealing a pattern of good works, with a doctrine of integrity (see Titus 2:7).

The Church should set the standard when it comes to integrity and godly character. We are encouraged not to conform to this world but be transformed, thus becoming agents of change. Many people want to conform and it shows in their choice of a *non-threatening, non-challenging* church environment, but the power of God is in transformation. You cannot stay the same once you encounter Jesus Christ. I encourage everyone to worship in an environment that stretches you and compels you to change and grow.

6. You will have single focus

"The light of the body is the eye, and if the eye is single, the whole body will be full of light." [Matthew 6:22]

So many people live complicated lives, attempting to juggle and prioritise the various facets. When you have your eye on the Cause, all those things fall easily into place according to a single vision.

Instead of compartmentalising your life, allow the Cause to become the single thread that connects the different facets of your life.

The Apostle Paul spoke of "This *one thing* I do … ." I am often asked how I do all the things that I do, but really all I do is one thing – I am a Church builder. All the responsibilities and activites of my life are connected to that single theme.

7. You will become successful

Success is a Bible word. The Lord promises that the Word will enable you to make your way prosperous and give you good success (Joshua 1:8). This involves meditating on the Word, living according to its principles and obeying the commandments of the Lord.

Some people think that the Lord will wave a magic wand and they will prosper. The reality is that God wants *you* to build His principles into your life so you can be successful – and it is not success based solely on self, but on making a difference and impact on others.

The world won't necessarily understand and 'religious' people won't like it, but when the Word is working in your life, not only will you prosper, but the Church will too. The healthy soul of the Church is built according to the healthy lives of the people.

Every cause will have an effect, so be prepared: When you live for the Cause, its effect will be evident in every area of your life, and in turn begin to affect the lives of others. The Cause goes well beyond yourself.

PART 2

LIVING
FOR THE CAUSE

CHAPTER SIX
CHOOSING LIFE

'I HAVE COME THAT THEY
MAY HAVE LIFE,
AND THAT THEY
MAY HAVE IT TO THE
FULL'

– Jesus Christ
[John 10:10 (NIV)]

CHAPTER 6

CHOOSING LIFE

I once saw someone wearing a T-shirt that said: "Everyone who lives dies, but not everyone who dies has lived." You may know someone like that who is on a journey to that end – someone who is empty, hopeless and depressed. To them, life is a bland existence – to be endured, rather than enjoyed.

From the moment you were conceived, you were given life. So what are you going to do with it? Life is all about choices and the subsequent consequences that follow. When God created mankind, He gave us the will to choose and make decisions – even the choice of whether or not to have God in our lives.

Many gathered to observe the crucifixion of Jesus Christ and stood looking on. The sad thing about human nature is that it so often likes to sit back and observe instead of actively taking part. You cannot be *neutral* about the Cross because there is no middle ground – you have to make a choice.

The Bible tells us to choose this day whom we will serve. If you choose God then you cannot stand passively among the crowd. One way or the other, you need to choose where you stand. You cannot hope to succeed by being a friend to worldliness for six days and then expect to encounter God's presence on Sunday.

When Jesus hung on the Cross and gave His life for mankind, He gave up His right to choose. He said, "Not My will but Your will be done." He then died for the Cause. The Cross has since forced every human being to make a choice: to accept Him or reject Him.

The first people to make that decision were the two criminals who hung on crosses on either side of Jesus. The incident is reported in Luke 23:32. Both were condemned to death, but one chose to blaspheme and reject Him. The other chose to accept Him. It was to this man that Jesus gave the assurance that he would be with Him in paradise that very day. That thief may have lived a sinful life, but in his last moments, he made the greatest choice of all: accepting the King and His Kingdom.

Jesus lived a powerful life committed to the Cause and, in spite of rejection, betrayal and persecution, He never swayed from His purpose. It was the Cause that empowered His ministry, enabling Him to declare with absolute conviction that:

"The Spirit of the Lord is upon Me, because [*or for this cause*] He has anointed Me to preach the gospel to the poor; He has sent Me to heal the brokenhearted, to proclaim liberty to the captives and recovery of sight to the blind, to set at liberty those who are oppressed; to proclaim the acceptable year of the Lord." [Luke 4:18,19]

Life is for living and Jesus declared that He came so that we could have abundant life. Living for the Cause is all about *choosing life* in all its fullness and living every day for that purpose. As a believer, a revelation of the Cause goes beyond your own salvation, but includes the powerful dimension of bringing His world to this world. Choosing the Cause is choosing life and living a life that goes well beyond youself.

CHAPTER SEVEN

SLEEPING, EATING AND WORKING FOR THE CAUSE

'EVERY DAY
IT'S YOU I LIVE FOR'

– Lyrics from *Everyday*
[©2000 Joel Houston/Hillsong Publishing]

CHAPTER 7

EATING, SLEEPING AND WORKING FOR THE CAUSE

During a visit to Sri Lanka in 1980, I stopped to watch a Hindu procession winding its way through the streets. It astounded me to see how people tortured themselves physically for the sake of their religious beliefs. A number of them had driven spikes into various parts of their bodies, but there was one gruesome scene that still remains in my mind. A man had strung himself through his flesh from an A-frame on a cart, and hung suspended on what looked like butcher hooks.

The Apostle Paul instructed us to present our bodies as a living sacrifice, holy and acceptable to God (Romans 12:1). Giving yourself as a *living sacrifice* doesn't mean you have to put your body through such agony and torment. That same verse translated in the Message Bible says, *"take your everyday, ordinary life – your sleeping, eating, going-to-work, and walking-around-life – and place it before God as an offering."* What it really boils down to is allowing the ordinary aspects of your life – your sleeping, eating and work – to become part of your daily commitment to Christ.

You may look at well-known people who preach the Gospel to tens of thousands in crusades all over the world. It is easy to think that living for the Cause is measured by such great events and occasions. But those events are merely the *fruit* of a lifestyle committed to the Cause. God has a great plan for your life, and a life committed to serving God and the Cause is built on the *small, everyday things*.

There is no doubt that Jesus lived so that *every day* of His life was occupied with the Cause. Some days involved preaching to large crowds, other days were one-on-one encounters, and there were also times He escaped the multitudes and sought God alone. And so our reason for living for the Cause is encapsulated in the way we approach *every day*. In fact, it comes right down to the ordinary things of life: sleeping, eating and working. Let me explain.

SLEEPING FOR THE CAUSE

You are probably wondering how your sleep can serve the Cause. Doesn't sleep mean that you are doing nothing? Not at all. You can only go a certain amount of time without sleep before you become unproductive. Sleep is God's way of renewing, restoring and replenishing our bodies, so that we can be alert, energetic and effective for what we are committed to do.

After an exhausting, busy day, a good night's sleep will recharge you for the next day. According to the Word, the promise of God is that our sleep should be sweet – not ridden with anxiety and fear.

"When you lie down, you shall not be afraid; you shall lie down and your sleep shall be sweet." [Proverbs 3:25]

A good night's sleep equips us to serve the Lord effectively. I certainly enjoy my sleep, but I also enjoy being awake. After all, life is for living, not sleeping. We need to rest but we aren't called to embrace the sleeping patterns of slothful people. There are those who waste a lot of time lying around in bed and others who miss great opportunities because they are asleep to their potential and are oblivious to the possibilities awaiting them. There are also those who, because of their sleepy state, don't notice the warning signs that their relationship is in trouble until it is too late and thereby miss the opportunity to rescue it.

"Do not love sleep, lest you come to poverty." [Proverbs 20:13]

The Word warns us about becoming a sluggard whose lazy lifestyle revolves around sleep. In Proverbs 6:6, it instructs us to look at the ways of an ant. Well, I haven't spent a lot of time observing ants, but I do have two dogs. They seem to sleep with one ear up, always mindful of what is going on around them. No matter how often I have tried to sneak up on my sleeping dogs, they are always alert to my presence.

Don't be a sleepy Christian who misses God's revelation or opportunity. Sleep is essential for our well-being, and necessary to equip us to serve the Lord, but surrender to the Cause of Christ by having disciplined habits.

Sleeping isn't your right but a means of giving your body as a sacrifice – it contributes to the purpose of serving God. There may be times when your sleep becomes an offering to the Cause. Our staff and volunteers often run on four or five hours sleep during our annual Hillsong Conference because of the pace of the conference, but they do so without complaint. Why? Because it is all for the Cause and that, in turn, energises and equips them to go the extra mile.

Put your sleep in perspective. It is *not an escape from reality*. It is designed to recharge you so that you can arise each morning and live for the Cause of the King and the Kingdom.

EATING FOR THE CAUSE

How do you eat for the Cause of Christ? Do you feast or do you fast? I know people who have fasted for 40 days. They lost so much weight that their clothes hung off them and then they battled to get back into a normal eating pattern again. Of course there may be times when God instructs you to fast, but to simply fast with a mentality that assumes God will bless you is ill-advised.

On a physical level, there are those who develop eating disorders because they are hung up about food and the way they look. Ultimately food rules their life. Others are emotional yo-yos, binging on anything they can find in the pantry when they feel depressed. This obviously stems from deeper issues.

I don't believe that God has a problem with food or eating – heaven is even described as a banquetting table. Sitting around a table and sharing a meal with friends or family is one of life's great pleasures. In the Garden of Eden, God told Adam he could eat freely from any nourishment, but some have become strict and religious about it. While the Old Testament contains numerous dietary laws regarding food, we are liberated from the law under the New Covenant. The Apostle Paul wrote:

"For the Kingdom of God is not about food and drink, but righteousness, peace and joy in the Holy Ghost." [Romans 14:17]

Your commitment to the Cause of Christ is not about how much, how little or what you eat, but about developing a healthy attitude to food. In the same way that a good night's rest recharges you, food provides nourishment, energy, strength and even enjoyment. Our bodies need fuel to function properly so we can be effective in our service to God.

Eating for the Cause shouldn't give you an excuse to become a glutton, because eating is merely a means to an end. Always determine your motivation for eating.

In his second letter to the Thessalonians, Paul wrote about freeloaders and those with disorderly conduct. He concluded by saying:

"If anyone will not work, neither shall he eat." [2 Thesselonians 3:10]

Many people live empty, unfulfilled lives because eating is such a big issue to them. For those who are busy-bodies, a meal is an opportunity to gossip, revealing their critical, cynical nature. For others with a low self-esteem or poor self-image, mealtimes are a frightening experience because it confronts the disorder of their life.

Instead of being ruled by food, see food from a Kingdom perspective. If you are committed to the Cause, you need to develop a healthy attitude to food, recognising that eating is a means of fulfilling your Kingdom purpose.

WORKING FOR THE CAUSE

In an era where the traditional nine-to-five working day has ceased to exist, and where technology has increased the capacity of one's ability, it is important to know *why* you are working and *what* you are working for. It is the will of God that you should work, but not to be over-loaded to the detriment of the other aspects of your life. If your sleep, eating patterns and relationships are suffering, you may need to put your work in perspective.

Jesus said:

"Come to Me all you who labour and are heavily laden, and I will give you rest." [Matthew 1:28]

He spoke of work and rest in the same sentence. Ultimately the two should compliment each other. The Cause of Christ can take the toil out of your labour, particularly when you see your work in terms of Kingdom purpose.

"Do not labour for the food which perishes, but for the food which endures to everlasting life, which the Son of Man will give you." [John 6:27]

What are you working for? Having no purpose or sense of direction can cause you to fall victim to the stress and pressures of work. Many others work as a means to reach their own goals, pursuing wealth or success as the answer to their hunger. There are certain things you cannot live without, and the promise of God is that by putting the Kingdom first, all these things will be added to you (see Matthew 6:33).

Instead of labouring for the wrong reasons, begin to see what you do in terms of serving the Lord. Let your job, your business or your studies be directed towards building the Kingdom, and you will find that your work will energise and stimulate you. Toil and heaviness disappear when your work relates to the Cause.

"Therefore, my beloved brethren, be steadfast, immovable, always abounding in the work of the Lord, knowing that your labour is not in vain in the Lord." [1 Corinthians 15:58]

When you work with a Kingdom spirit, your attitude will change your atmosphere at work and make a difference.

A life consumed with the Cause of Christ will be a life that goes beyond yourself. When you are committed to the Cause of the King and the Kingdom, your eating, your work and your sleep all have higher purpose. It is when you begin to see these ordinary, everyday details of life in terms of your commitment to the Cause, you will discover a powerful, extraordinary way of living.

CHAPTER EIGHT

PARTNERING FOR THE CAUSE

'HERE IN THIS HOUSE
OF THE GREAT KING
WE'VE COME TOGETHER NOW
TO WORSHIP HIM'

CHAPTER 8

PARTNERING FOR THE CAUSE

God's business is all about people. The Cause of the Cross is to connect people to God, and then connect people to each other. I believe there are *God-inspired connections* and these occur throughout the course of one's life.

I find myself connected in relationships on various levels. Apart from the intimate relationship I share with my wife, I enjoy partnership with my staff, my team of the executives in my denomination, my ministry friends around the world, as well as my personal friends, my children, and my community contacts ... and the list could go on. Naturally, strong, godly relationships are essential for us to fulfil the Cause of Christ, and it is a revelation of the Cause that will, in turn, make us choose good partnerships.

Throughout life, you will find yourself connected in various levels of relationships. Those you attach yourself to, or align yourself with, will either advance or obstruct God's plan for your life. You cannot live in isolation and expect to prosper, so it is important to understand the value of partnership and allegiances, both spiritually and naturally.

The Bible is full of instruction and wisdom regarding relationships. According to Proverbs 18:1, a man who isolates himself seeks his own desire. Those who prefer to live detached and isolated are usually self-focused and self-centred. They are seeking their own agenda and own interests.

The Bible also says that *two are better than one* and goes on to explain why: they will have a good reward for their labour (see Ecclesiastes 4:9). Teamwork enables us to achieve so much more. Solomon continues to promote the concept of two being better than one because of the support that is engendered. If you are in danger of stumbling, be it physically, emotionally or spiritually, you have someone who will lift you up.

He also says that partnership will keep you warm (see Ecclesiastes 4:10). This is obviously true in the context of a bed, but look beyond the physical level to the spiritual and emotional warmth that companionship provides.

Finally, there is greater strength when people stand together, because 'though one may be overpowered by another, two can withstand him' (see Ecclesiastes 4:12). On your own, you are easily overtaken, but a partnership is an infinitely more powerful force.

It is important to have affinity and partnership in the right areas so that you can move into all God has called you to. There are many people who have embarked in partnerships but have been hurt in the process. Possibly someone let them down or didn't play their part, and because of that experience, they are hesitant to trust again.

God's will is that partnership will be a great blessing in your life, but pervert it even slightly and those involved experience a lot of pain. Within every partnership is a seed that has the potential to produce fruit of either great blessing or destruction.

When God puts something together, it has a divine destiny and will always bear fruit. When a couple get married, the covenant pronounces over their lives "what God has joined together, let no man put asunder" (Mark 10:9). It would be foolishness to break up what God has put together, be it a marriage or any other partnership, but on the other hand, you don't want to try and put something together that God never intended to join together either.

First and foremost, it is God's plan and purpose that you are in partnership with Him. To be effective for the Cause of the King and the Kingdom, you also need to be connected to a Church and be in fellowship with other Christians.

"From whom the whole body, joined and knit together by what every joint supplies, according to the effective working by which every part does its share, causes growth of the body for the edifying of itself in love." [Ephesians 4:16]

Going solo in life minimises your strength and capacity, and one of your permanent partnerships should be your attachment to the Body of Christ. While your partnership with God and His Church are positive alliances, you need to be careful when it comes to making decisions about the other partnerships you enter into. The Bible is clear that light and darkness cannot fellowship together and produce something good.

There are elements of partnership that need to be understood and applied in order to build strong, godly relationships. Partnership is all about sharing. Because human nature can be selfish, many people don't want to know about this. The blessing of partnership isn't meant to restrict so that you have less, but genuine partnership always means there is a greater reward and something more to enjoy. Kingdom Partnerships will always add more to your life.

SHARED CONTRIBUTION

Partnership is all about shared contribution. You have to put something into a partnership to make it work. It is about receiving and contributing. It takes two to live in a marriage partnership. There are many marriages which are not joined or connected in the way God intended – they may be living together as man and wife, yet they are not experiencing the power and blessing of the marriage partnership.

My wife, Bobbie, leads the 'Hillsongwomen' meetings every week. One day she felt an urgency to pray for those who had great need in their relationships, and asked them to anonymously write down their requests. Sadly, the most common request written was 'that my husband would love me.' The cry of most women was for true intimacy and love.

Look at Leah, the first wife of Jacob. He woke up in the morning and

71

discovered he had been tricked into marrying the wrong woman. But see it from Leah's point of view:

> "When the Lord saw that Leah was unloved, He opened her womb; but Rachel was barren. So Leah conceived and bore a son, and she called his name Reuben; for she said, "The Lord has surely looked on my affliction. Now therefore, my husband will love me." [Genesis 29:31,32]

The cry of her heart was simply to be loved by her husband. She hoped that the children she bore to Jacob would bring love into the relationship, because even though they were legally married, they were lacking the affinity of partnership.

That same cry is within so many people today, who are feeling unloved and unhappy in their relationships. They are not experiencing the power of affinity or intimacy, and are not enjoying the blessing of partnership because their relationship lacks commitment to contribution. Contribution is more than just lip service, it comes from the heart. Sowing into someone's life requires you to open up and have a certain degree of vulnerability.

SHARED EQUALITY

Partnership recognises equality and because leadership exists in every relationship, there will also be leadership in partnership, but that doesn't mean that one is better or the other is subservient.

There are those who have perverted what the Bible says about submission in terms of godly marriage and godly leadership, and because of that, they don't recognise this equality. God made us all different, with various roles in life, but He also made us all equal.

> "For I do not mean that others should be eased and you burdened; but by an **equality**, that now at this time your abundance may supply their lack, that their abundance also may supply your lack – that there may be equality." [2 Corinthians 8: 13,14]

Equality is essential for a good partnership. In business, a true partnership means you share risks, costs, profits and losses. It is not about one person taking all the risk and the cost, while the other person enjoys all the profit.

Marriage is an equal partnership based on 'for better, for worse, for richer, for poorer.' This does not mean things get better for you while they get worse for your partner! Nor does it mean richer for you and poorer for them! If you have two cars in the family, who drives the 'bomb' is significant because equality is all about wanting to see your partner blessed.

The spirit of partnership is one that shares the load because you both partner in the vision. In any kind of relationship there has to be that sense of equality and contribution.

SHARED COMMITMENT

Partnership is about commitment and faithfulness. Jesus used the illustration of the unfaithful steward, saying:

"And if you have not been faithful in what is another man's, who will give you what is your own?" [Luke 16:12]

If you can be faithful in what belongs to another person, God will give you the opportunity to be faithful over your own. When you get married, you are literally taking responsibility for someone else, and the commitment is 'to death us do part.'

Some partners are fiercely independent and their personal interests are much greater than their combined interests. A spirit of faithfulness will build partnership and we need that spirit of commitment if we are to know the great blessing of partnership.

SHARED PURPOSE

Purpose and vision unites people and brings a sense of rallying together. Partnership depends on shared purpose. God will put people in our lives because of His predesigned purpose. It is often when we lose sight of this purpose that we lose that sense of partnership.

For instance, a young couple who are building a house together may work overtime to make their dream happen. All their enthusiasm and energy is generated into this one purpose. Yet after they have moved into the house, all of a sudden, cracks begin to appear in the relationship. What happened is that somewhere along the line they *lost their shared purpose*.

Where there is a lack of purpose, things begin to fall apart. You need to have true, united purpose in your marriage and other relationships. If there is a lack of purpose, there tends to be a lack of partnership as well.

It is always a tragedy when those in high profile ministry positions lose perspective and put themselves before the Cause of Christ. The impact of a broken marriage is destructive, resulting in a great deal of pain for all involved. Ultimately it weakens their effectiveness for the Kingdom.

When one's eyes are on the Cause, it is amazing what doesn't matter, but put one's eyes on self, and it is amazing what begins to matter. When someone begins to fantasise about what life would be like without their partner, they open the door to a deception about freedom. Sadly, those who follow through on those delusions find that instead of the dream of freedom they envisaged, it often ends up a nightmare of loneliness and lost opportunity.

I have no doubt that if Bobbie and I lost sight of the Cause, we would begin to drift apart and find reasons why we were no longer compatible. But we have made a conscious decision that such choices are unacceptable, and are committed to maintain our vow that 'until death do us part.'

It is interesting that when you cut off all the options, your love becomes stronger. Keeping your eye or focus on a single cause is crucial for marriage partners.

Living for the Cause goes beyond you and it means building godly partnerships that will bear great fruit. Not only will they enhance and bless your life, but they will be part of fulfilling God's plan and purpose for your life, empowering us to make a greater impact for His Kingdom.

CHAPTER NINE

UNITED AROUND A CAUSE

'IN THIS PLACE DREAMS
ARE MADE
IN THIS PLACE WHERE
YOU ARE'

CHAPTER 9

UNITED AROUND
A CAUSE

Every year, I do several ministry trips with the Hillsong worship team to various cities and towns all over the globe. I am truly blessed with an awesome team who are faithful and committed to the Cause – people like Mark and Darlene Zschech who have worked alongside Bobbie and me for many years and are also among our closest friends.

Yet we are also a mixed bunch of personalities. After a couple of weeks of travelling, eating and living together, like all other human beings, we have had moments when we can become a little irritable. But we get over those moments easily, and won't allow it to affect our team. What keeps us united? The Cause of the King and the Kingdom!

WHAT CORDS BIND YOU TOGETHER?

Partnerships and alliances are formed because of common interests, goals or a unified purpose. During World War II, the allies of Britain united together because of a common enemy. That was the element that brought and held them together.

The Word says that a threefold cord is not easily broken (see Ecclesiastes

4:12).When you plait a rope with three strands, it is much stronger than a two-fold cord. Every partnership and relationship has three strands to it. Firstly, there is you; secondly, there is your partner (or partners), and thirdly, there is the *thread of common interest* that brings you together. It is this third strand that ties the relationship together.

Having a common purpose adds great strength to a relationship, but there are times when people join together for negative, destructive reasons. After Jesus was arrested, He became a political hot potato, so to avoid making a decision, Pilate sent Him to Herod. This was the result:

"That very day Pilate and Herod became friends with each other, for previously they had been at enmity with each other." [Luke 23:12]

Prior to that, Pilate and Herod had been enemies, but they united together over a common cause: their contempt for Jesus. You see the same happening with young people, who normally wouldn't like each other, but the cord that unites them together is rebellion or anger towards their parents or 'the establishment.' Even in church life, someone who is negative and critical will be drawn to others with similar feelings, and unite together because of their common grievances.

The power of any relationship is what holds it together. The key is to build the right third cord into every relationship and partnership. Godly vision and purpose binds people together.

Love is another cord that binds together our intimate relationships, such as marriage. The Word says that love hopes all things, endures all things and never fails – so this cord has a 100 percent guarantee. Without love, a sense of hopelessness will lead you to give up. That is usually when marriages head for the divorce courts. One of the most destructive cords in any good partnership is a third party who adds a wedge into that relationship. If the enemy has the opportunity to destroy a godly partnership, you can be sure he will.

Every one of us has the potential to include the greatest third cord in our relationships: Jesus Christ. When He becomes the cord that ties your partnerships together, be it in the home, the church or in business, you can be confident that something strong and fruitful will be built out of them.

Look at the most powerful partnership of all – the Trinity. The Father, the Son and the Holy Spirit complement each other perfectly and work together as one. When you give your life to Christ, you are not only living for Jesus, but you have a powerful opportunity to partner with Christ.

"And they went out and preached everywhere, the Lord working with them and confirming the Word through the accompanying signs."

[Mark 16:20]

That's what partnership is all about, working together in unity, with Kingdom purpose and Cause. God puts us together with others so we can be more effective. When people ask me what is the greatest dynamic of my working relationship with our worship team, I know that it is our relationship and wholehearted commitment to building the Church. It isn't a solo effort and we need each other to do it. Like everyone else, we have opportunities to feel hurt or annoyed with each other, but instead of becoming distracted by minor things, it is the Cause that unites our team together.

When you are united for the Cause, it is amazing what doesn't matter and what you don't even notice. It is when people begin to take their eyes off the Cause and live for themselves that they become negative, cynical and critical. They begin to look at 'what he said' or 'what she said' and make other issues a priority. Self interest and potential offence joins the equation and momentum is lost.

MARRIAGE

Right from the beginning God said that it is not good for man to be alone. Marriage and intimacy was His idea! The breakdown of a Christian marriage is always a tragedy, but when it happens, it isn't so much about irreconcilable differences, nor the issue of finances or even unfaithfulness. I believe it happens because they lose sight of the Cause that brought them together.

When the Pharisees asked Jesus about the case for divorce, they were attempting to trap Him with doctrine. Yet when Jesus answered, He focused on the real issue: the reason to stay married.

And He answered and said to them, "Have you not read that He who made them at the beginning 'made them male and female,' and said, 'For this reason [*for this Cause*] a man shall leave his father and mother and be joined to his wife, and the two shall become one flesh?' [Matthew 19:4,5]

Jesus put things in perspective by going right back to the beginning and describing God's original concept of marriage. Yet it goes a lot further than the creation of a man and a woman. He went on to say in verse six that "what God has joined together, let not man separate." According to God's plan and purpose, He made them and for the Cause, He joined them together. It is the Cause that strengthens a marriage partnership because it unites two people together for a powerful reason.

When I first met Bobbie (my wife-to-be) I told her that I wanted to be a pastor and a church leader. At that time, I had no idea how big this dream would be and how it would impact our lives. We knew it would come with a cost and would have its sacrifices, but we built our relationship around the Cause. We have had our challenging moments, but our marriage is firmly grounded on the Cause. With that as our focus, the other little issues don't matter because our priority is the Cause.

FRIENDSHIP

One aspect of living a prosperous life in God is to know the blessing of friendship. A friend is someone you love and consider dear. Sadly, some miss out on that, because they are over-powering, over-possessive and self-orientated in their friendships. Others put their friendships in overdraft by continually withdrawing from them, but never investing anything in.

There are those who sit on the fence, trying to be everyone's friend and end up being a friend to no-one. A loyal and trusted friend will make a clear choice to stand with you in good times and tough times. They won't listen to idle gossip by busy-bodies who talk behind a friend's back. They won't use or abuse you, but will add something into your life.

How far would you go for a friend in trouble? Jesus said that there is no greater love than to lay down your life for a friend.

"You are My friends if you do whatever I command you. No longer do I call you servants, for a servant does not know what his master is doing;

but I have called you friends, for all things that I heard from My Father I have made known to you." [John 15:14,15]

Serving God and living for the Cause is a great honour and privilege in life, but Jesus doesn't call us servants – He calls us friends. Servants are there to do things for you, but a friend is so much more. He is the one who will never leave you or forsake you, and He is the one who sticks closer than a brother (see Proverbs 18:24).

Jesus was called a friend of tax-collectors, publicans and sinners. It doesn't mean He was yoked to them, but He was a healer of their lives.

The power of any relationship is the cause or reason that binds it together. When you are united with Jesus, your friendships will be built around the Cause, and the foundations of your relationships will be held together by the principles of God.

CHAPTER TEN
REJECTING THE MIDDLE GROUND

'I'M NOT CONTENT JUST TO WALK
THROUGH MY LIFE
GIVING IN TO THE LIES
WALKING IN COMPROMISES'

– Lyrics from 'Believe'
[© 1999 Donna Lasit/City Bible Music]

CHAPTER 10

REJECTING THE MIDDLE GROUND

One thing about human nature is that it likes to play it safe. Many people don't like to choose sides so the middle of the road seems like the safest place to be. The reality is that sitting on the fence doesn't get you anywhere, and if you stay in the middle of the road, you will inevitably get squashed!

The connotations of 'middle' imply mediocre, bland and lukewarm. Why live your life in an indifferent, neutral state of grey when there is so much more? Many opt for the middle ground not realising that it is actually the lowest ground in the Kingdom of God. If you want the Cause to be the foundation of your life, then it demands that we reject mediocrity and the middle ground.

The middle ground is the lowest ground

In the natural, we may see things and rate them in the order of high, then middle, with low at the bottom of the scale. But look at it this way: when you are high or low, you are somewhere specific, but the middle is usually a state of limbo.

You may argue that there is nothing wrong with playing it safe, but if you want to experience and achieve great things in your life, the middle ground is not the place to be. In a spiritual context, the middle ground is actually the lowest ground.

The middle ground lacks progress

If you have ever driven a manual car with a gear shift, every time you change gear you will always pass neutral. The other gears will all put you in a position to go somewhere (forwards, and even backwards), but neutral is the one position where you end up going nowhere. You cannot have the car in neutral and expect to go forwards.

You can expect the same in your life. You cannot be neutral about your commitment to Christ and expect to enjoy the rewards. You cannot expect Bible promises if you refuse to live by Bible principles.

If you stand for nothing, you'll fall for anything. As a believer you will need to make a stand for the gospel because that is where the power and mobility is. If you don't make a stand, you will certainly fall by the wayside and never go forward. The power, progress and momentum in your Christian life comes from taking a stand.

The middle ground lacks purpose

In Australia, we experience mid-summer in the month of January. It was 40 degrees celsius one summer day when I left Sydney to preach at a leadership conference in Munich, Germany. In that kind of heat, anything cold has a purpose! Nevertheless I arrived in Munich in mid-winter on a day when the temperature gauge was reading *minus* 21 degrees celsius! In those freezing temperatures, anything hot has a purpose!

Both hot and cold have a valid purpose, but lukewarm is mediocre and purposeless. Jesus compared our Christianity in terms of temperatures.

> "I know your works, that you are neither cold nor hot. I could wish you were cold or hot. So then, because you are lukewarm, and neither cold nor hot, I will vomit you out of My mouth." [Revelation 3:16]

You can spot a 'hot' Christian immediately. They are those on fire and passionate about the gospel. But as Jesus indicated, even one who is cold is preferable to someone who is lukewarm and has no purpose. So in that sense, the opposite to hot is not cold, but lukewarm. Lukewarm is unpleasant and distasteful to Him. Hot and cold involve specific choices, but lukewarm plays it safe in the middle and avoids making a choice.

In a natural order, we see things in terms of hot, progressing to lukewarm and finally, cold. We see lukewarm as the middle ground but Jesus puts lukewarm as the lowest ground. Lukewarm Christianity puts you in a rut, and according to one definition – a rut is a coffin with the ends taken off.

The middle ground lacks friends

There was a time when a couple who were close friends of Bobbie and I were going through a painful divorce. I would have preferred to sit in the middle and not take sides, but one party was making choices that would hurt their church. As a leader in the body of Christ, I knew I needed to decide where I would stand.

When it comes to relationships, we have to choose where we stand. The Bible says that 'the man of many friends (a friend to all the world) will prove himself a bad friend, but there is a friend who sticks closer than a brother' (Proverbs 18:24 [AMP]).

Someone who tries to be a friend to everybody prefers to be neutral and uninvolved. They end up being nobody's friend, because true friendship has to make choices.

In life, you will have loyal friends, neutral acquaintances and possibly a few enemies. The way human nature would order relationships would be friends as the high ground, neutral acquaintances in the middle, and enemies as the lowest ground. But look at it this way: your loyal friends will stick with you in times of adversity, and support you in times of trouble. You may know who your enemies are, but there is no point in losing sleep over them. Even your enemies cannot ultimately hurt you, but *a disloyal friend can.*

During his prison term, PTL founder Jim Bakker was asked if he had lost any friends. His answer was profound: "No," he said, "I simply found out who my friends really were."

In times of trouble and adversity you need friends who will not remain neutral. To be a good friend, you will need to make choices about where you will stand. My experience is that most good friends will want to do this so that in a time of crisis, you can count on them standing with you.

The middle ground lacks faith

I have vision and faith to see our new church building completed and filled to capacity. It is an enormous challenge, but we wouldn't be increasing or progressing as we are without a significant measure of faith.

The Word declares that 'the just shall live by faith, but if anyone draws back, My soul has no pleasure in him' (Hebrews 10:38). Faith looks ahead in expectation of the unseen possibilities, but a 'safety first' mentality will never give faith a chance. Instead of going to another level, they will draw back.

Naturally we would think of *faith* in terms of the high ground, and doubt as the lowest ground, with a *cautious safe approach* in the middle. But even doubt is better than refusing to move. Like Thomas, the disciple said, "I'll believe it when I see it," doubt is open to persuasion and change.

Some areas of the Church have become anaethetised by playing it safe and not making a stand in faith. If you want to live a fulfilled, purpose-driven life in Christ, you will need to make a stand and step out in faith.

The middle ground lacks passion

Making a stand involves taking a side and feeling passionate about a cause or an issue. It will involve a certain degree of emotion, but far better to love or even hate, than to have *complete indifference*. Those who feel nothing but indifference are actually coming from the lowest ground.

In a later chapter, we will examine the power of passion. Don't settle for the middle ground and a bland, ordinary and indifferent existence. Decide to feel passionate and enthusiastic about life, eager to be involved.

The middle ground lacks respect

Those who take the high road put God first in everything they do, the low road does nothing, and those who take the middle road do things half-heartedly. The Word is clear that half-hearted is worse than doing nothing at all.

Paul wrote how God loves a cheerful giver, and encouraged us to give generously, not out of obligation or necessity (see 2 Corinthians 9:5). Sometimes doing nothing is better than doing something with the wrong attitude. In the books of Acts, Ananias and Sapphira lied about what they were giving, while they had kept some for themselves. It would have been better if they had given nothing at all. God respects that which is given to Him first, from a willing heart, but rejects that which is done because of obligation or grudgingly which ultimately is the lowest ground.

In a later chapter, we will examine the importance of priorities and what it means to put God first in your life.

The middle ground lacks life

There are only two choices before us, according to the Word: life and death (see Deuteronomy 30:19). God doesn't offer us a bland existence as a middle ground option. Jesus promised that He came that we may have abundant life (John 10:10). That abundant life is not a middle-of-the-road existence.

Like a marriage relationship that is in trouble, you cannot ignore the problems and just co-exist together. You are faced with choices: to work at it or accept the inevitability of seeing the demise of the relationship. You will need to do something and take a stand.

If you long to live a life of purpose where you desire to experience the fullness of God, you cannot compromise by settling for the middle ground. There will be times when you will be unpopular and other times when you will face persecution, but the price is higher when you settle for the middle ground.

Living for the Cause demands you address the inclination to settle for the middle ground and make a stand.

CHAPTER ELEVEN
LIVING WITH CONVICTION

'YOU LIFT ME ABOVE MY FEARS AND SET MY FEET ON SOLID GROUND'

CHAPTER 11

LIVING WITH CONVICTION

A general election or referendum on a particular issue can be a fascinating exercise in observing human nature. In the weeks prior to the election, weekly opinion polls begin to reflect which way voters are swaying. There will usually be a number of hardcore voters who stand firmly on each opposing side, but the swing of balance is usually focused on those who haven't quite made up their mind. As the debate heats up, these are the voters that each contender aims to influence and persuade to vote for their cause. They are an unknown, uncertain entity who often don't know where they stand because they don't have any firm convictions.

The truth is that if you stand for nothing, you will fall for anything. Too many people don't know what they really believe in life. They have no firm convictions or solid persuasions so they aren't committed to anything in particular. Their instability and double-mindedness tosses them backwards and forwards.

Your convictions are the beliefs and persuasions that ground you and establish the pattern of your life. One can only admire those who make a stand for what they believe in, or live for a specific cause. In April 1994, South Africa held its first democratic, multi-racial elections and Nelson Mandela was elected president of his country by a vast majority. Yet more than three decades before, he had made a stand and went to jail for 27 years for the cause he believed in – the struggle to end apartheid in South Africa.

I know, I believe, I'm committed, I'm persuaded

On any given Sunday, millions of Christian believers attend church services all over the world. How many would be prepared to be arrested and jailed for their faith? The Apostle Paul was one who was prepared to go to jail and suffer persecution for the sake of the gospel. The Apostle Paul was able to say with absolute conviction:

> "For this reason I also suffer these things; nevertheless I am not ashamed, for I **know** whom I have **believed** and am **persuaded** that He is able to keep what I have **committed** to Him until that Day." [2 Timothy 1:12]

It is Paul's fervour and persuasion that have inspired others over the centuries to commit to the Cause of Christ. He knew, he believed, he was persuaded and he was committed. There are many who don't know their convictions and are unsure what they believe. The result is that they can be easily persuaded and they aren't committed to anything, when they could be influential and persuasive.

Your persuasion cannot be separated from the pattern of your life. Where and how you stand will set the course of your life. Paul went on to exhort and encourage Timothy to 'Hold fast the pattern of sound words which you have heard from me.' Whatever your convictions in life are, they will set the pattern of your life.

If you have strong convictions, you will have a strong life, but if your convictions are weak and wavering, your life will be the same. Those who stand for nothing will live according to a pattern of inconsistency, going from crisis to crisis. Yet those who stand on the promises of God see a pattern of blessing in their lives.

You can build a pattern in your life that will produce God's blessing, but you will need to make a stand. The choices and decisions you make for the sake of the Cause determine your convictions. When it comes to the cross of Jesus Christ, you cannot look on – you have to make a stand. There is no middle ground.

To be *in* the world or *of* the world

Many believers wrestle with the balance of living *in* the world and being *of* the world because it seems to be a paradox. For instance, the Apostle Paul commented on our relationship with the world, saying:

"Do you not know that friendship with the world is enmity with God? Whoever therefore wants to be a friend of the world makes himself an enemy of God." [James 4:4]

Here Paul warns against being a friend of the world, yet Jesus was called the friend of tax collectors and sinners. We are also cautioned not to love the world (1 John 2:15) but the Word says for God so loved the world ...' (John 3:16).

Here is another apparent paradox: 'Come out from among them and be separate, says the Lord' (see 2 Corinithians 6:17) but Jesus told us that we are salt and light to the earth (see Matthew 5:13).

We are all born into the world and live within its sphere, but we do not have to be conformed to the world's substance – i.e. its mentality and value system. A life committed to the Cause of Christ will impact and influence the world, rather than the world influencing and impacting you. It doesn't mean living in exclusion but we know (or should know) where our feet are firmly planted.

Jesus successfully balanced living *in* the world while not being *of* the world, and our challenge as believers is to do the same. The shallow values of the world didn't influence Him, but rather He had a dynamic influence on those who looked to worldly pursuits.

To live with conviction, you need to choose whether you will live *in* or *of* the world system.

To live by conviction or consequence

One of the differences between being *in* the world and *of* the world is living by conviction or by the consequences. Ever since I was a young boy, I knew deep down that I was born for the Cause. My convictions affected my thinking, directed my choices and set the pattern of my life. This included my decision to go to Bible College and study for ministry, as well as my choice of my partner. I am not just married to Bobbie; I know that she and I are called to be together for God's purpose. Our conviction for the Cause of Christ has cemented our marriage so that we stand together and hold fast to the Word. This establishes the pattern of a long and happy marriage.

But if you have no convictions, you will have poor standards and suffer the consequences. When facing tests and trials, how will you stand fast?

The Bible says:

"Most men will proclaim each his own goodness, but who can find a faithful man?" [Proverbs 20:6]

The majority of people will look at what is good for them, compared to those who faithfully look at what is good in the eyes of God. The Word also says:

"There is a way that seems right to a man, but its end is the way of death." [Proverbs 16:25]

Living with conviction means you live according to the ways of God, while living by consequences revolves around what you think is good for you. It boils down to what *is* right and what *seems* right.

The key to living with conviction is faithfulness and a commitment to the principles of God. These attributes set a standard and a pattern for your life. No matter what happens in life, you need to have convictions about your faith, your marriage and even the church you belong to. You need to be able to stand firm when tough times come, knowing what you believe and where you stand.

To conform or to transform

The advent of Sydney Christian Life Centre in 1977 flew in the face of the accepted mindset of the time. There was a general air of skepticism about Sydney and the potential to build a strong church there. Other Australian states, such as Queensland and South Australia, were seeing infinitely more growth and the prevailing thinking was that Sydney was a 'graveyard for preachers.' Glory be to God that Sydney CLC became an agent of change, and the result is that the spiritual landscape of Sydney is very different today. Now there are great churches thriving across the city.

The Apostle Paul encourages us not to 'be conformed to this world, but be transformed by the renewing of your mind' (Romans 12:2). Don't be 'of' the world, conforming to its mold by taking on worldly rationale, cynicism and values. Rather hold fast to your convictions and see your life transformed, and let your convictions begin to impact others. The word 'infested' means to be inhabited or overrun in dangerous and unpleasantly large numbers. In that context, our Christianity should be infesting the world. It is God's will that you become an agent of change *in* the world.

The disciples of Jesus became dynamic agents of change, and the scriptures describe them as turning the world 'upside down' (Acts 17:6). Likewise, the Apostle Paul was criticised in his time for persuading 'men to worship God contrary to the law' (see Acts 18:13).

It is very easy to conform to one's upbringing or the way things have always been done. Tradition or conservative values that are passed down through generations keep people bound, but it will take conviction to break out of the comfort zone and establish a new pattern and environment.

For instance, if someone is diagnosed with a life-threatening disease, they can either conform to the predictions of the medical reports, or they can stand with conviction that it is God's will to heal them. One who stands in faith will have more power and strength working in their life than those who submit to the world's rationale.

To worship the creature or the creator

The Bible is very clear about specific issues, but those who have no convictions about God and His Word are blind to the truth. Humanism, post-structuralism and New Age thinking have allowed absolutes to disappear, so people have no convictions or little to hold fast to. Sadly, there are even those who spend years in theological college but end up so intellectual about the scriptures that they don't recognise God's power or revelation. Such people attempt to lock God out of His own house.

The Apostle Paul wrote of these:

"who exchanged the truth of God for the lie, and worshipped and served the creature rather than the Creator." [Romans 1: 22-25]

The question is: Is it all about Him, or is it all about you? There are two certainties in life. Firstly, there is a God. Secondly, you are not Him!

When life revolves around the creation instead of the Creator, you have materialism, instead of prosperity. It is all about receiving, instead of giving. With no convictions it is easy to become swallowed and engulfed by the world's mediocrity and poor thinking.

When your convictions are built on God's Word, they establish a strong foundation on which you can live out the Cause. Decide to make a stand and live with convictions that will establish the pattern and path of your life.

CHAPTER TWELVE

A LIFE OF PASSION

'I'M LIVING FOR THE TRUTH …
THE HOPE OF THE WORLD
IN YOU I'LL STAND'

CHAPTER 12

A LIFE OF PASSION

In September 2000, over fourteen thousand world-class athletes arrived in Sydney for the first Olympic Games of the new millennium. Having spent years in preparation and training, they all had one goal in mind: to win an Olympic Medal. An attitude of indifference or apathy to their sport didn't bring them to that point of their career. It was a deep passion within that inspired a level of commitment and determination that had spurred them on to succeed.

Many Olympic visitors to Sydney attended our weekend church services during the Games, including a number of athletes who are not only champions in their particular sport, but champion the Cause of Christ in their personal lives. One such athlete is Penny Heyns, a South African breast-stroke swimmer who, among many achievements, won Olympic Gold in Atlanta in 1996, and broke an incredible eleven world records. She helped make arrangements so that during the week I had the opportunity to enter the Olympic Athlete's Village and lead Bible Studies and pray with them. Among those who attended were Gold Medal champions and successful athletes from several countries. I was inspired by their single-mindedness and determination in their sport, but I became very aware of their personal vulnerability and anxieties.

I love people who are passionate about life and what they are doing. They are usually the ones who succeed and achieve great things. To live a full and effective life committed to the Cause, you will need to understand the power of passion.

LOVE, HATE, INDIFFERENCE

What do you think is the lowest ground when it comes to passion? Most people may think the opposite of love is hate, but I believe indifference is far worse. I am certainly not advocating hate, but being lukewarm or indifferent will ultimately rob you of passion and limit your potential. Love and hate involve strong feelings of emotion and passion, but indifference doesn't care.

Within the context of a marriage, indifference is a sad state of affairs. Take a couple who were once starry-eyed and built their relationship on strong emotions of love and passion, but over time it begins to break down. Now hate is a strong emotion, but even lashing out in anger can be less painful than cold indifference? It is tragic when one partner is able to walk away feeling absolutely nothing but indifference to the whole partnership. Instead of notes on the pillow or romantic love letters, their communication is limited to basic necessities: "John, it is your turn to have the kids this weekend. Pick them up at 4pm from school. Mary."

Jesus taught a message of passion inspiring us as Christians to be passionate about God and life itself. Apathy or mediocrity will rob you of the awesome life He has in store for you. Some have a picture of Jesus Christ as meek and mild, but He always spoke with passion and conviction. In fact, some of the things He said were extremely provocative and challenging. Jesus spoke a lot about love, but He also used the word 'hate' on occasion. Naturally Jesus doesn't hate anyone, but by using such strong terms and instructing us to hate something Jesus was emphasising a specific point.

Indifference robs us of potential

As it is written,"Jacob I have loved, but Esau I have **hated**."

[Romans 9:13]

We know that God so loved the world that He gave His Son, so how can God hate anyone? I believe He hated what Esau stood for – an attitude of indifference to the blessing and promise of God – while his brother Jacob had set his heart on obtaining the promise of God.

If you read the story told in Genesis 25, Esau came in from a day of hunting and hungered for the stew that Jacob had cooked. He willingly agreed to give his birthright to his brother for some food, and as the Bible describes it, 'Esau despised his birthright' (Genesis 25:34). He was completely indifferent to the fact that his birthright was his potential, his future and God's plan for his life. That indifference caused him to miss out on the blessing of God.

Here is another occasion where Jesus instructs us to hate:

"If anyone comes to Me and does not **hate** his father and mother, wife and children, brothers and sisters, yes, and his own life also, he cannot be My disciple." [Luke 14:26]

Instead of taking a scripture out of context, we need to read it in line with everything Jesus said. The tenor of this teaching was to love, honour and respect others, so the word 'hate' is exceptionally strong in this sentence. I believe He used such strong language as an idiom to make a point. We have all done it at some stage. For instance, after a very energetic workout at the gym, we say, 'I'm dying!' or when we are running late for a meal, we say, 'I'm starving!' Of course we aren't really dying or starving, but we exaggerate it to make a point.

Jesus certainly wasn't instructing us to hate our families in the context of malice and ill-will. The word is used in terms of making a strong comparison. Other translations of the scripture have put it this way: "If you *prize less dearly* …" or as the Living Bible puts it: "If anyone does not love Me *far more* than he does his own father … ."

Prior to this, Jesus had told the parable of a great feast. The invited guests all made excuses about why they could not come, and it is in the context of such indifference that He spoke. He continued to speak about the cost of carrying your own cross and following Him. Indifference and disinterest will keep you from living your life effectively for Christ's Cause.

Here is another statement Jesus made about hate:

"He who loves his life will lose it, and he who **hates** his life in this world will keep it for eternal life." [John 12:25]

Jesus wasn't talking about someone who was depressed and suicidal, but rather someone who was indifferent to Christ. One who loves their own life and excludes Jesus will lose it, but one who lays down their own life for His sake, will gain it.

The power of balance

How can you rise above apathetic indifference and mediocrity in your life? One way is to know the power of balance. Becoming balanced isn't about calming down when one is extreme or radical, nor is it about becoming less passionate and mediocre. The power of balance is all about giving attention to everyday things with as much passion across *the whole spectrum* of your life.

On one occasion, Jesus spoke to the Pharisees about tithing. They were passionate about tithing because they were fastidious about the Law. Yet they were indifferent to the love, mercy and justice of God. Jesus cautioned them about their absorption with various tithes to the exclusion of other things, saying:

"These you ought to have done, without leaving the others undone."

[Luke 11:42]

There are those who are passionate about the church but neglect the needs of their family, their marriage, their health and finances. They wonder why they lose them down the line. It is not a matter of becoming less passionate about the church, but becoming as passionate about every area of life. You can be passionate about serving God in church seven days a week, but not to the detriment of other important aspects of your life.

Our multiple church services over the weekends require my full attention, but on Mondays I have had to learn to switch off. This is the day when I focus on other things in my life – like sweeping up leaves in the garden, playing with my dogs or enjoying a café latté with my wife or good friends. It doesn't mean I am any less passionate about the purposes of God.

I have identified seven areas that we should never leave undone. Give attention to all these areas and avoid becoming indifferent to them. Always keep the following in balance:

• Your spiritual walk and relationship with God.

• Your family.

• Your social life and ability to enjoy life and have fun.

- Your career, your work or your business.

- Your friendships and relationships.

- Your physical needs and your health.

- Your ministry – those areas you have committed to serving God

This list isn't ordered in any priority because you need to show passion right across the balance of your life. The Apostle Paul teaches us to 'walk worthy of the calling with which you were called' (Ephesians 4:1). This word 'worthy' literally means balanced.

Know the power of passion in every aspect of your life. Don't only be passionate about your work, but balance that with the ability to know when to switch off and give attention to other things. When you go on holiday, enjoy it with all your heart. Certainly do not feel guilty about how you are serving God through that holiday because it is enabling you to be much more effective in the weeks and months to come.

Demotivators that breed indifference

I heard a tale about one guy who was asked, "What is the biggest problem in the Church today – ignorance or apathy?" He replied, " I don't know and I don't care!" The power of indifference is in its disinterest and demotivation. To move forward, we need passion.

Jesus addressed the church in Ephesus, saying:

"Nevertheless I have this against you, that you have left your first love." [Revelation 2:4]

When you leave something, it isn't taken from you – you choose to leave it behind. A man who *loses* his wife to a terminal disease is different to a man who *leaves* his wife.

In order to live a life full of passion, you need to recognise those things that will breed indifference, including those that rob you in your spiritual walk.

Offences

At some point you will be hurt and offended by someone, and initially this may give rise to some strong emotions. However, holding on to offences will gradually cause you to become indifferent and detached.

Paul wrote of the root of bitterness which could spring up (Hebrews 12: 5). Offence and bitterness will always affect your perspective on life, so don't allow your hurt and offence to develop roots that sink in and take hold.

Disappointment

When things don't happen as we expect them to, we may feel a twinge of disappointment. But when you allow that disillusionment to set in, it can lead to indifference and cynicism. The way to prevent it is endurance. The Word says:

> "For you have need of endurance, so that after you have done the will of God, you may receive the promises." [Hebrews 10:36]

God sees what you have sown, and He promises that in due season you will reap. Keep your expectations high.

Sin

The weight of sin will ensnare you and quench your passion for God. Don't allow it to hold you down, but confess your sins to Him, repent and continue to walk forward in freedom and forgiveness.

Relationships

Always choose carefully your source of advice or counsel. If you are facing marriage problems, it isn't wise to receive advice from someone who is coming from the perspective of their own failure. The counsel that will emerge from their position of bitterness or hurt is probably not what you need to be hearing. If you are looking for sympathy, you will be drawn toward people who identify with the problem, yet Christ-like compassion will point toward answers.

Jesus was full of passion – He had a passionate love for God, a zeal for lost people and fervent desire to do God's will. He went to the Cross because of His passion, for the sake of the Cause. Imagine if He was indifferent to it all? Indifference will never cause you to live a fulfilled life of purpose for the Cause of the King and the Kingdom.

CHAPTER THIRTEEN
FIRST PRIORITIES

'I'M REACHING FOR THE PRIZE
I'M GIVING EVERYTHING
I GIVE MY LIFE FOR THIS
IT'S WHAT I LIVE FOR'

– Lyrics from '*Faith*'

CHAPTER 13

FIRST PRIORITIES

You can have a great vision or dream for your life, and you can have convictions that you believe in. You may even be on fire and passionate about the Cause of the King and the Kingdom, but unless you give His Kingdom first place, your life will be empty and unfulfilled.

One of the greatest compliments I ever receive is when people tell me that they can see that I live what I preach. Is what you are saying the same as what you are living? There are those who profess to be Christians, but when the time of testing comes, they fall apart. Your life is held together by your convictions and your priorities.

"He is before all things, and in him all things hold together."
[Colossians 1:17 (NIV)]

If Christ isn't your priority, then your life can become unglued. There are Christians who fall apart emotionally because they put worry and anxiety before trusting in Him. Others wonder why they face continual financial problems but instead of putting the Kingdom first, they give out of their left-overs. If two people put God first, they will stick together and their marriage is likely to hold fast no matter what happens.

Regardless of the challenges that face you, your life will unfold according to a certain pattern. Those whose priorities are centred around the Cause will see the rewards of their commitment emerging in their life. The pattern of your life will be determined by your priorities or what you deem important.

These priorities will be formed according to a number of things:

• Your *convictions* (what you believe) will cause you to stand fast in tough times but if you are not convinced, you will get lost in times of testing.

• Your *desires* (what you want in life) will also determine your priorities. You will always give attention to the things you value in life. Jesus said:

"For where your treasure is, there your heart will be also."

[Mattthew 6:21]

• Your *vision* (what you see for your life) will also establish what is of primary importance in your life. So will your *affections* (what you love) determine what you commit to.

Living for the Cause means you will know where you stand, and what your convictions are. Therefore, you will be passionate about what you believe in. The Cause and everything associated with it will become your priority. The Apostle Paul's priority was clearly the Kingdom of God. He was prepared to go to prison for what he believed in.

You will know if Christ is genuinely your priority by what comes FIRST in your life. Take for instance, your time. Think about where you direct most of your time. Does your work or business absorb all your attention? How about television or sport? None of these things are bad but if they take first place, they are determining your life's impact. How about your thought patterns? Does God occupy your thinking, or do you say a quick prayer when you need a quick answer?

What about your speech? You cannot separate the words of your mouth and the meditation of your heart. The Word declares:

"Let the words of my mouth and the meditation of my heart be acceptable in Your sight." [Psalm 19:14]

You can easily determine what is important in my life by what I talk about. I have no difficulty holding a conversation about sport as it is one of the loves of my life. A good outlet, but not my first priority. Our words and confession will reveal our priorities in life.

FIRST THINGS FIRST

The story is told in Genesis 4 how Cain and Abel brought offerings to the Lord. Abel didn't hold back with his offering and gave the Lord the firstborn of his flock, but Cain gave Him his left-overs. Sometimes doing nothing is better than doing something half-heartedly. The outcome was that God accepted Abel's offering but rejected Cain's.

The principle of first fruits is a powerful spiritual truth because it determines the position of God in your life. It also activates the promise and blessing of God. Jesus spoke about a number of things that we need to put first and how they will affect our lives.

Harmony in your relationships

"Therefore, if you bring your gift to the altar, and there remember that your brother has something against you, leave your gift there before the altar, and go your way. **First** be reconciled to your brother, and then come and offer your gift." [Matthew 5:23,24]

Someone who is angry and wants vengeance for their hurt, may attend church, praise God and give financially, but will wonder why they don't have the blessing that the Bible promises. Their bitterness will infect the other areas of their life – this is why Jesus instructs us to first reconcile and get our relationships right. Don't allow anyone else to rule your spirit because the time and energy you spend in strife and anxiety will only shrink your life. Whether you have issues with your family, your boss or any other acquaintances, make it a priority to resolve it and move on.

A non-judgmental spirit

"**First** remove the plank from your own eye, and then you will see clearly to remove the speck from your brother's eye." [Matthew 7:5]

People have a tendency to be harsh and critical of others, but Jesus taught us the pitfalls of having a judgmental spirit towards others. Sadly this is the pious way many Christians live. Imagine the reality of having a wooden plank extending from your eye. Think of all the damage you would do as you moved around, knocking things over and bashing people in the head every time you turned. It would affect the way you would see life, seriously limit your accessibility, and would be a major obstruction in your relationships. Think about all the places you couldn't go because of that plank.

Jesus advises us to first take a look at what is in our own lives before we condemn others. Decide to live with a positive, encouraging spirit which believes the best of people, instead of criticising or judging them.

Reduce your degree of vulnerability

"How can one enter a strong man's house and plunder his goods, unless he **first** binds the strong man? And then he will plunder his house." [Matthew 12: 29]

The enemy is always 'seeking whom he may devour,' but is he able to? Jesus gave us all authority and He taught us the need to bind him. The Greek word for bind means to 'curb his powers.' Some Christians will scream and shout as they attempt to bind the devil, quoting scriptures and claiming victory. But the best way is to live according to the Word of God. If you are living according to the principles of God, attacks may come but the Word will protect you.

Some believers end up becoming targets for the enemy because they don't seal the backdoor. The enemy will aim for you but you need to cut off the angles. Give him no place, no opportunities, no permission and no advantage.

Confront internal issues

"Woe to you, scribes and Pharisees, hypocrites! For you cleanse the outside of the cup and dish, but inside they are full of extortion and self-indulgence. Blind Pharisee, **first** cleanse the inside of the cup and dish, that the outside of them may be clean also." [Matthew 23:25,26]

Jesus was never one to mince words and He made His point clearly: you first need to deal with things on the inside. You can wear a Hugo Boss suit, have an impressive career, a beautiful wife, a fancy car and a huge Bible, but the external image doesn't count. It is what's on the inside that really matters.

A world-famous supermodel, Niki Taylor, was in a car that jumped a curb and plowed straight into a pole. She was wearing a seat belt and seemed to escape serious injury as she got out of the car with her famous visage unscathed. But by the time the police arrived she was in terrible pain and emergency room doctors soon discovered she was suffering from massive internal injuries. This is a physical example of a spiritual reality.

The mess on the inside of your life won't disappear if you cover it up with a glamorous façade. Eventually it will begin to destroy you from the inside because it will rule your life. Don't leave your emotions, your attitude or your thinking unchecked. Let God begin to work in your heart and clean you up from the inside.

Do your homework

"For which of you, intending to build a tower, does not sit down **first** and count the cost, whether he has enough to finish it." [Luke 14:28]

You probably know people who are great starters but lousy finishers. Jesus taught us the value of counting the cost first because there will always be obstacles to overcome.

Every year, a new intake of students start Bible College. Having heard from God, they are usually full of zeal and excitement about their destiny and future. But as the months go by, you find one or two begin to drop out because they find it too hard. The Lord didn't change His mind – these are usually the ones who didn't count the cost before they started.

Before we began building our new church building at Hillsong Church, we counted the cost – not only the financial costs, but the spiritual, physical and natural costs. If we hadn't approached the project this way, we may have been beaten by the first snag. But by God's grace, the various ministries of our church have never been impeded by the building programs.

There will always be challenges and obstacles in life, but Jesus promises that whoever loses their life for His sake would gain it. It is up to us to run the race and finish our course. Success comes when we put the Kingdom first. Jesus told us to:

"Seek **first** the kingdom of God and His righteousness, and all these things shall be added to you." [Matthew 6:33]

If we hold fast to His priorities and to those things He told us to put first, we can know the abundant life God has promised us. It is all about putting the Kingdom **first.**

PART 3

DYING
FOR THE CAUSE

CHAPTER FOURTEEN
TO DIE FOR

'FOR WHOEVER
DESIRES TO
SAVE HIS LIFE WILL
LOSE IT, BUT
WHOEVER LOSES HIS
LIFE
FOR MY SAKE
AND THE GOSPEL'S
WILL SAVE IT'

– Jesus Christ
[Mark 8: 35]

CHAPTER 14

TO DIE FOR

In recent years I have found that I spend a lot of time in airports and aeroplanes, either departing to or arriving from some speaking engagement. I once sat down and worked out that in one year I caught almost 200 planes. That works out at about one plane journey every 48 hours. Besides accumulating a lot of frequent flyer points, it also puts me in a high-risk group. My wife Bobbie once sat next to a man on an overseas flight who was adamant that he would never take a sleeping pill on a plane because he wanted to be awake if anything went wrong. To be honest, I'd rather be asleep if anything did.

Our days are numbered and life on earth is destined to end one day. Have you ever wondered how you will go, because there are quite a few different options? I knew of a wonderful old preacher, P B Duncan, who never settled for retirement. He was still preaching the Word in his eighties. Then during a Sunday church service, he finished preaching his last sermon and the congregation began to sing an old song "Within the veil I now would come, into Your holy place to see Your blessed face ..." and he did! What a way to go!

When your eye is on the Cause, you don't have to fear death, because you already have confidence about eternity. The Apostle Paul expressed what death meant to him: 'For me to live is Christ, to die is gain.' He lived for the Cause and he was prepared to die for the Cause.

A revelation of the Cause of Christ not only establishes the reason why you were born and the purpose for living, but the Cause also relates to death and dying. If you know what you are living for, you will inevitably know what you are prepared to die for. Jesus often spoke about laying His life down for the Cause and willingly gave up His life for it. The power of the Cause in your life is persuasive. It determines your priorities, establishes your convictions and sets your standards. It becomes your passion, just as the death and suffering of Jesus is often referred to as His passion. At Easter, depictions of Christ's sufferings are called 'passion plays.' The passion of Jesus is as relevant today as it was almost 2000 years ago when He died on the cross.

First of all, His passion was towards the Father. His love for God dominated His life, so that everything He did revolved around serving and glorifying Him.

Secondly, His passion was for lost people. Jesus said, "I am the good shepherd. The good shepherd gives His life for the sheep" (John 10:11). Over the centuries, millions have responded to the message of the Gospel and been reconciled to Christ.

Thirdly, His passion was to do God's will. In the Garden of Gethsemane, He prayed:

"O Father, if it be possible, let this cup pass from Me, nevertheless not my will, but Your will be done!" [Matthew 26:39]

Jesus was always 'about His Father's business' – in both life and death.

A passion for God and His Cause will ensure that the major focus of our Christianity is not self, but to love Him, to reach others and to do His will. We are not saved purely for selfish motives, but we are saved and called for a purpose that goes beyond ourselves. If we build our lives around doing His will, we can put aside those things that draw us away from the Cause.

The Cause will give your connection to the world a purpose that will affect your family, your work, your finances and your relationships. It will even affect what you lay aside and are prepared to die to … for His Cause!

As a baby, you are dependent on others for your needs to be met, and your entire focus is on self. Sadly, some people never graduate beyond that stage and they become adults who are completely self-centred and self-absorbed.

Which side are you on?

We may say, if someone is peckish, they aren't starving but a little on the hungry side. If someone is biggish, they aren't huge but on the larger side. So if someone is selfish, they are on the side of self.

When we talk about *self*, we are referring to the flesh and the ego. *Self* occupies the part of *you* that Christ wants to occupy, and *self* will try grimly to hold on to its position.

When *self* comes into the picture, the purposes of God get confused. His incredible plan and purpose for *you* is blessing and prosperity. The Word has some awesome things to say about *you*:

> "For I know the thoughts that I think toward *you*, says the Lord,
> thoughts of peace and not of evil, to give *you* a future and a hope."
> [Jeremiah 29:11]

Here is another:

> "And try Me now in this," says the Lord of hosts, "If I will not open for *you* the windows of heaven and pour out for *you* such blessing that there will not be room enough to receive it." [Malachi 3:10]

Whenever you see the word '*you*' in the Bible, put your own name there. The promises are for YOU!

Whereas God thinks *you* are awesome, *self* is destructive. *You* thrive in the presence of God, but *self* thrives in the absence of God. *You* have limitless potential, but *self* merely has limitations. *You* are human but *self* is humanist.

While the Bible has numerous promises of blessing and prosperity, it also warns us about *self*. Paul wrote that where 'envy and *self-seeking* exist, confusion and every evil thing are there' (see James 3:16). The purposes of *self* are directly opposed to the Cause of Christ.

> "For men will be *lovers of themselves*, lovers of money, boasters, proud,
> blasphemers, disobedient to parents, unthankful, unholy, unloving,

unforgiving, slanderers, without self-control, brutal, despisers of good, traitors, headstrong, haughty, lovers of pleasure rather than lovers of God."

[2 Timothy 3:2-4]

To live for the Cause of Christ requires dying to *self*, but *self* will always try to exalt *itself*, striving towards its own desires. Ultimately *self* will sabotage the purposes of God. Those who are prepared to die to *self* are those who reach the place where they have chosen to not only live, but die for the Cause, and in effect, build the Church of Jesus Christ.

CHAPTER FIFTEEN
DYING TO SELF

'SO WE LAY DOWN OUR
CAUSE THAT
OUR CROSS MIGHT BE
FOUND IN YOU'

– Lyrics from '*Believe*'

CHAPTER 15

DYING TO SELF

S ometimes we have a funny way of describing things that when you think about them, don't really make sense. Have you ever told anyone:"Leave me alone. I want to be by my*self*!" How can you be by (or next to) your *self*?

Or what about when you are feeling extremely anxious and worried about a particular situation, and you tell someone, "I was beside my*self*?" I'd like to see you get beside (or alongside) your *self*. In truth, *you* and *yourself* are not the same thing.

Having read the preceding chapters of the book, you will have realised that you were born for the Cause, and have the capacity to do great works for the Cause of the King and the Kingdom. So what on earth can stop you?

Believe it or not, the greatest enemy of the Cause of Christ is your *self*!

We all start off life being ruled by *self*. I remember driving our family to a specific destination with one of our babies screaming their lungs out the entire journey. Obviously something was upsetting our child, causing him to be unhappy with him*self,* and at that moment, there was no consideration for anyone else in the car.

Self will try to hijack you

The Word says that God breathed into *you* the breath of life – it didn't say He breathed the breath of life into *self.* Self attempts to confuse the two, so that people don't understand the difference between *you* and *self.* Self will make you feel guilty about God's blessing. There are many Christians whose lives are small and insignificant because they keep trying to lay down '*me*' instead of '*self.*' Something has to die, but it is not *you.* You need to be alive so that the Lord can effectively use you. The part that has to die is *self.*

The Word says:

"I have been crucified with Christ; it is no longer I who live, but Christ lives in me; and the life which I now live in the flesh I live by faith in the Son of God, who loved me and gave Himself for me." [Galatians 2:20]

Self will shrink you

While God's plan is to enlarge and expand *you, self* will begin to shrink you. Being *self*-conscious means you are aware of *self.* When I first started preaching, I was *self*-conscious: I spoke too fast and never knew what to do with my hands. I kept wondering what everyone was thinking. I shrunk my whole consciousness down to me, when the realm of Christ is so much bigger. When 'Christ in you' begins to impact your life, He opens you up to a much bigger world enabling you to see beyond your*self.* If someone is self-conscious, we advise them to "be yourself." But don't be your*self – self* is the problem. Be *you,* because *you* are awesome.

Self has limitations

A talented musician may claim to be *self*-taught. That's certainly admirable, but his or her gift will be limited by self. Instead of going to lessons and allowing someone else to teach them more, they will be unable to go beyond a certain level.

A *self*-confident, *self*-taught or *self*-made person can seriously limit their potential. The natural ability of a great athlete will only take them so far, but those who compete at the top level, usually have a team of experts surrounding them. People whose role is to help them reach out beyond them*selves* and conquer previously unattainable levels.

The Word says that a fool is *self*-confident (Proverbs 14:16) but that doesn't mean we shouldn't have any confidence. Paul instructs us not to throw away our confidence (Hebrews 10:35). He didn't say *self*-confidence because he is talking about the confidence which comes from the absence of self.

Self operates by stealth

Self will always camouflage itself, and attempt to hide itself in your spirituality, humility or compassion. My second book, *You Need More Money*, is interpreted by some as *Self Needs More Money*, because they read it from their position in life – the position of *self*. The main thesis of the book is about attracting finance to your life so you are able to be an agent of resource and blessing to others. It is all about looking beyond your*self*, and having the ability to meet the needs of others.

Sadly, *self* has often disguised itself within the context of religion and spirituality, causing people to criticise or judge others harshly. It can even use scriptures to keep people contained, such as 'whoever exalts himself (or his *self*) will be abased, and he who humbles himself (or his *self*) will be exalted' (Matthew 23:12). The reality is that God's desire is to see you lifted up – it is not to downgrade or suppress you. It is a matter of taking *self* out of the equation. To humble yourself literally means to make *self* low.

Self will preoccupy you

Someone who is ruled by the past events or tragedies of their life may be preoccupied or consumed with *self*. Telling them to forgive themselves won't help. Forgiveness always releases and sets free, but you need to be rid of *self*. There needs to be a mercy killing. I suggest you let *self* die and the feelings of guilt and condemnation will die with it. Then, as you allow Christ to occupy that same part of you that your *self* previously occupied, *you* will come alive. It is no longer *self* that lives but Christ that lives in *you*.

The trend may be to 'self-talk' for motivation and inspiration. The truth is you do need to talk to your *self* – but in a different context. You need to tell your *self* exactly what the Word says. Instead of believing in your *self*, believe in the

Lord Jesus Christ. Instead of justifying *self*, *you* are justified by faith. Instead of *self*-control, *you* need to be controlled by the Spirit.

Self will always dominate and preoccupy your life with the focus on it*self*. If you desire to serve the Cause of Christ, you will need to '*self-destruct!*'

CHAPTER SIXTEEN

ON THE ROAD
TO SELF-DESTRUCTION

'I LAY DOWN MY LIFE INTO YOUR HANDS'

–Lyrics from '*For This Cause*'

CHAPTER 16

ON THE ROAD TO SELF-DESTRUCTION

S acrifice is one of those words that probably makes you feel uneasy because it carries connotations of pain, but anything worthwhile always comes at a price. Waking up before the sun rises to go for a run may not be pleasant, but the reward will be a sense of accomplishment and commitment to gain a fit, healthy body. You need to look beyond the sacrifice and see the advantages and rewards.

In Romans 12, the Apostle Paul tells us to present our bodies as a living sacrifice, and be transformed by the renewing of our minds. You can be assured that when you choose to lay down your life for the Cause, your *self* will rise up in protest. The Bible tells us that the carnal mind is at enmity with God, so you can expect conflict between your godly desires and the ambitions of your *self*.

"For where envy and *self*-seeking exist, confusion and every evil thing are there." [James 3:16]

The Word says that where self-seeking exists, the result is confusion and evil. When *self* is involved, what God intended to be a powerful blessing in life becomes distorted and confused. Significant aspects of life, such as money, sex and power, all of which God intended to be a blessing to you, become confused and perverted by the insatiable appetite of *self*.

Money

"For the *love of money* is a root of all kinds of evil, for which some have strayed from the faith in their greediness, and pierced themselves through with many sorrows." [1 Timothy 6:10]

Money itself isn't evil, but the love of wealth and finance leads to destruction. To *self*, money becomes a master, but to *you*, money will be a servant. Finance with Kingdom purpose is an awesome resource that can bless others.

Always remember that if you see a need and have nothing, then there is nothing you can do. If you have a little, you can help a little, and if you have a lot, then there is a lot you can do. Free from the shackles of *self*, money has a great deal of potential. Christians who react to such teaching are coming from a *selfish* perspective and certainly not thinking about others.

Sex

"Flee *sexual immorality*. Every sin that a man does is outside the body, but he who commits sexual immorality sins against his own body."
[1 Corinthians 6:18]

Each year, Sydney hosts a huge Gay & Lesbian Mardi Gras parade through the city streets. It began in the Seventies as a protest march for gay rights, but today is merely a visual display of sexual gratification.

To *self*, sex is all about the gratification of its own needs, but when Christ is in *you*, sex is all about fulfilment and is focused more on fulfilling your partner's needs above your own.

Sexual immorality leaves its mark on individual's lives – broken relationships, hurt, distrust and bitterness. The Word instructs us to 'exercise *self*-control' (see 1 Corinthians 7:9). The reason *self* needs to be confronted is that in the pursuit of *self*-gratification, it perverts sex and turns a potential blessing into a curse.

We need to control the demands of *self*, and desire the marriage union to be the blessing God intended. Instead of being all about 'me' and 'my' desires, sexual intimacy should be all about fulfilling the needs of your partner.

Power

"You shall receive *power* when the Holy Spirit has come upon you; and you shall be witnesses to Me in Jerusalem, and in all Judea and Samaria, and to the end of the earth." [Acts 1:8]

The promise of God on the day of Pentecost was the power of the Holy Spirit. When power is connected to Kingdom purpose, it will have an influence and impact on the lives of others, yet a confused, distorted concept of power is when *self* seeks power for its own ends. You may have observed seeming control freaks who, driven by *self,* love to control and manipulate others.

By God's grace, our church has had the awesome opportunity through praise and worship to impact nations with the Gospel. If our motives were *self*-seeking, we would probably have self-destructed. Darlene Zschech has attained world-wide recognition as our worship leader. By now, if she was focused on *self*, her ego would keep demanding more for her, and less for the Kingdom. She would be talking about 'me' and 'my gift,' yet she is still the same gracious, humble lady whose heart has always been to worship and glorify God.

Self will always pursue fame, power and success relentlessly, but Christ in *you* will see the enormous value of influence and opportunity for the sake of the Kingdom.

Love

"*Love* does not behave rudely, does not seek its own."
[1 Corinthians 13:5]

At some stage you may have read the renowned chapter on love in 1 Corinthians 13. Everyone has a need to love and be loved, but there are those who confuse love by thinking it is all about indulging *self.* Just as sex can become self-seeking, so can some people's concept of love. In the Kingdom, the character of love is revealed in its generosity and giving.

You will see how *self* distorts the blessing of love if you read 1 Corinthians 13, replacing the word 'love' with 'self.' Notice how the promise loses its impact when focused on *self.* The Word says that love does not seek its own, but *self* will always seek its own (verse 5). Love will never fail, but the cause of *self* is guaranteed failure and destruction.

Happiness

"Happy are the people whose God is the Lord." [Psalm 144:15]

So many spend their life in the pursuit of happiness. To self, happiness is limited to a single moment or specific act, but when Christ is in *you*, happiness inhabits the majority of life. It can emerge in the midst of life's greatest challenge and triumphs. The key is His Lordship over your life.

A young, single person may think sexual encounters will add fulfillment or happiness to their life, but will merely discover the emptiness of sex outside the commitment and love of a marriage relationship.

In the elusive pursuit of happiness, so many people settle for a moment of pleasure, but end up with a lifetime of regret. Yet in the Kingdom, a moment of self-denial can lead to a lifetime of happiness.

Generosity

Jesus said it is 'more blessed to give than to receive.' *Self* loves to get but Christ in *you* will love to give. *Self* may want to be seen as generous, and will often give with strings attached. However a person with a Kingdom spirit will give with a pure heart and give regardless of whether it is seen or not.

When *self* is involved, spending is a lifestyle that gratifies oneself, and giving is seasonal. With Christ in *you*, spending is seasonal, but giving will be your lifestyle.

Leadership

Self will confuse true leadership, focusing on its own agenda and lording it over people. With *self* as a foundation, leadership is stymied by insecurity and 'strong' leadership becomes manipulative and controlling. With God at the helm, strong leadership is about example and the difference will always be evident in the fruit. A self-seeking leader will tend to 'use' people for their own means. Godly leadership gives others an example to follow and rather than crushing people, it enlarges and releases people.

All the promises of God are about *you*, not about *self*. When you lay down self, it is Christ in you that becomes the vehicle for Him to use.

CHAPTER SEVENTEEN
BUILDING THE CHURCH

'THIS HOUSE IS BUILT ON BUILT ON CHRIST OUR ROCK'

– Lyrics from '*Awesome in This Place*'

CHAPTER 17

BUILDING
THE CHURCH

O n a trip to Germany, I visited one of Munich's famous cathedrals. It was certainly an impressive architectural accomplishment, yet what I remember most about it was a box in the wall which contained a skeleton. Not a very inspiring, uplifting memory of a church, but the reality is that some churches are like that – full of dead people instead of the life of God.

I have spent all my life involved in church life and I would never change this for anything else in the world. I love what I do, especially the incredible honour of being a part of what Jesus said He would do – that is, building His church.

"I will *build My church* and the gates of hell will not prevail against it."

[Matthew 16:18]

People who say they love God but dislike the Church don't realise that they are despising the very thing Jesus loves and is committed to building.

Jesus was born for the Cause, He lived for the Cause and He gave His life for the Cause. The Church is God's plan for implementing His Cause – a cause that is empowered by three dynamic factors: (1) Jesus Christ, (2) the Holy Spirit and (3) the Church.

The gates of hell may try and keep people from a relationship with God, but Jesus promised that they will not prevail. Church is more than just a nice place for Christians to meet on a Sunday. I have seen people dislocate themselves from the church and open their lives up to all sorts of hell. Sowing yourself into building His Church will protect you from the ravages of hell.

DEAD RELIGION

The Church has the potential to be a powerful influence, but it is a tragedy when certain sectors of the Church lose sight of the Cause. Taking Christ and the Holy Spirit out of the Church causes it to become weak and ineffective. It is then little more than a social club.

Just like the old cathedrals of Europe, some churches end up as monuments to the past – cold and empty monoliths that once knew the life of God.

The Word says we are all temples of the Holy Spirit but some churches become temples of legalism and formalism. Instead of the freedom to worship God in spirit and in truth, the emphasis is on the ritualistic and legalistic religious procedures.

Some churches become huge hierarchical organisations, which struggle under the weight of their own structures. Others operate like corporations with stream-lined operations and sophisticated technology. I don't have a problem with innovation and entrepreneurialism within the Church, as long as it fulfills the purposes of the Cause. The truth is that buildings don't make churches. The Church is all about God and people.

The Greek word 'ecclesia' means 'the called out ones.' It is the will of God for the body of Christ to be a dynamic, living organism that in turn produces life. In the midst of our changing society, church growth experts have noted that certain sectors of the church are declining. Instead of a formal, ritualistic approach, churchgoers are wanting a freedom to express themselves in worship and receive Bible-based teaching that can be applied to their everyday lives. It is no coincidence churches that are truly exalting Jesus Christ and bringing the power of the Gospel in a relatable way are increasing and growing.

A PROSPEROUS CHURCH

Our church in Sydney is possibly Australia's largest congregation with over 12,000 members. As we grew bigger, we began to grow smaller at the same time. You may wonder what I mean. Every week, hundreds of cell groups meet in homes throughout Sydney, where people discuss the Word at a more personal level. These cell leaders, most of who have secular jobs, are committed to the Cause of Christ, and the building of His Church. Our vision to reach the city of Sydney is outworked through our city-wide network of cell groups, two major worship centres and contributing services and ministries. Instead of Bobbie and I having to pastor every member of our congregation, we have an awesome leadership team of staff and volunteers, who work alongside us, doing the work of the ministry. I believe this is why our church is alive, healthy and prospering.

According to 3 John 2, you prosper as your soul prospers. Because it is a living entity, at the core of a church lies its heart and soul. A prosperous church will have a healthy heart and soul. The prosperity of a church isn't only dependent on its worship, but worship is a reflection of what God is doing in the church. When people choose to lay down their lives and sow their gifts and talents into the local church, they add to its prosperous soul.

There are four significant aspects of the Cause of the King and the Kingdom that build a prosperous church.

Unity

The Word says that when people live harmoniously together in unity, there the Lord commands His blessing (Psalm 133:1). People may connect together for a specific cause but their relationships are often tainted with arguments and petty jealousies. When your eye is on the Cause, unity holds the team together so minor frustrations or irritations won't distract you.

Leadership

The pattern of the New Testament church is one of leadership, and a prosperous church will have great leaders who lead by example. As I've said before, any leadership skills I have acquired have been honed in church life. The enemy hates unity and good leadership, so attempts to distort it by pulling people down to size and keeping them contained. Remember, there is a big difference between worldly leadership which will try to crush and squash people, compared to godly leadership, which releases others.

Vision

A prosperous church will always have a great vision which is linked to the Cause. That vision will be outworked across every facet of church life, it will connect people in their relationships, and it will strengthen the foundations of the home.

Commitment

Another sign of a prosperous church is the degree of commitment among the people. Those who are prepared to die for the Cause will support the work of the ministry, giving of their time and talents, and sowing in their finances.

The Word encourages us to "serve the Lord with gladness" (see Psalm 100:2). For anyone in full-time ministry, either pastoring a church or overseeing any Kingdom work, it is a great honour and privilege to gladly serve the Lord and His Cause. But what brings added rejoicing is when you see people owning the vision, doing their part and committed to living a life of Kingdom purpose. Over the centuries, it has been those believers who were prepared to die to *self* who have built the Church of Jesus Christ and been effective in bringing His world to this world.

CHAPTER EIGHTEEN
ETERNITY IN YOUR HEART

'YOU SET ETERNITY IN MY HEART SO I'LL LIVE FOR YOU'

– Lyrics from '*Here to Eternity*'

CHAPTER 18

ETERNITY
IN YOUR HEART

At the turn of the new millennium, the New Year celebrations in the city of Sydney were broadcast to an estimated TV audience of three billion people all the over the globe. The countdown from 1999 to 2000 triggered off one of the greatest firework displays the city had ever seen, illuminating the city skyline, the Sydney Opera House and the Harbour Bridge. At the climax of the spectacular finale, a single word emerged in fifty-foot- high luminous letters on the bridge – 'Eternity.'

What a significant and powerful message for every human being across the face of the earth – the contemplation of eternity.

The story behind the word 'eternity' commemorated the life of a man who died at the age of 83 in 1967. Arthur Stace wasn't a history-making politician, nor was he a world-class athlete. He had virtually no education and from the age of 15, his criminal activities led to a succession of jail sentences. During the years of the Great Depression, he lived on handouts, and slid further down the road to alcoholism. Yet the story of his life is told all over the world today because of one single word that impacted his life – 'Eternity.'

In 1930 Arthur Stace found himself in a local church service and his encounter with God changed his life forever. It was the word 'eternity' that stuck in his mind and discovering a piece of chalk in his pocket, he felt compelled to write it on the pavement. For one who could hardly write his own name, he found he could write 'eternity' quite elegantly.

For the next 37 years, Arthur Stace would wake up early and after an hour's prayer, as God directed, he would write his word in chalk on the sidewalks of Sydney. Over the years, that one-word sermon became the object of much public speculation and curiosity as many contemplated its meaning.

Although it is a number of decades since Arthur Stace died, the evangelistic message of 'eternity' continues to live on, capturing the attention of another generation.

We, too, will all physically die one day, but what will we leave behind? Bear in mind, this side of eternity, we have *one opportunity* to choose how we live our lives.

IMPACTING FUTURE GENERATIONS

In my book *You Can Change The Future*, I wrote about impacting others and leaving a legacy as an inheritance for the generations to come. The reality is that as a Christian you are saved and called according to His purpose (2 Timothy 1:9) – to live a life that goes far beyond you. The choices and decisions you make in your life can impact and influence the lives of others. When God called Abraham to leave his hometown Ur, He had future generations in mind. The lineage of Abraham extended right through to Jesus Christ, and ultimately the blessings of Abraham are ours today.

Imagine if what Jesus Christ did on the Cross was only for those who lived in that time and who witnessed the events firsthand? As the crowds watched Him die on the cross in Jerusalem, God was looking far beyond. He saw people in the 1st century, the 10th century, and He even saw us in the 21st century.

The amazing grace and power of God's salvation continues to change and impact lives thousands of years later. The Gospel has been spread from Jerusalem to Judea to Samaria and to the uttermost parts of the earth, and continues to be passed on from generation to generation.

When Jesus was a young boy, His parents rebuked Him after they thought they had lost Him when He stayed behind in Jerusalem. Yet this is what He answered:

"Did you not know that I must be about My Father's business?"
[Luke 2:48]

The moment you join the family of God, you are called to be involved in the Father's business. No matter what job you may be employed to do, you need to see your work in terms of the Cause of the King and the Kingdom.

Every believer's business should exist to resource Christ's Kingdom. A mother looking after young children has Kingdom purpose: to train and raise up the next generation in the ways of the Lord and give them an awesome start in life.

So many people get caught up in the stress and pressure of their jobs, working to pay the bills and put food on their table, without seeing that their endeavours have the potential to build the Kingdom. The answer to a sense of futility in your work is to reposition your heart. The Word says this:

"He has made everything beautiful in his time; he has also *set eternity* in their hearts." [Ecclesiastes 3:11]

If you have eternity and Kingdom purpose in your heart, a mundane job of filing papers or digging a trench can be fulfilling. When your heart has a revelation of your contribution to the Cause of Christ, your work is far more than earning money to pay bills or wishing you could be doing something else. Instead of thinking about putting food on your table, with a Kingdom spirit, you begin to think about putting food on other people's tables. It is in seeing beyond yourself that you build a legacy for eternity by impacting the lives of others, and future generations, with the Cause of Christ. And that is really what dying for the Cause is all about: seeing beyond yourself with eternity in mind.

CHAPTER NINETEEN
YOU ARE MY WORLD

'YOU ARE MY WORLD
YOU ARE MY GOD
AND I LAY DOWN MY LIFE
FOR YOU'

– Lyrics from '*You are my world*'

CHAPTER 19

YOU ARE MY WORLD

At the start of this book, I spoke of the songs sung by thousands in the Homebush State Sport Centre in March 2000 when recording the 'live' worship album *For This Cause*.

A year later, in February 2001, our church hired one of Sydney's largest indoor venues, the Sydney Entertainment Centre, bringing thousands together for yet another evening of praise and worship, which has been recorded as the *You Are My World* album.

The new songs that emerge from the pens of our songwriters continue to reflect an unwavering passion for Jesus Christ and His Cause. To sing or to say "You are my world" is giving Him the highest honour and first place in your life. It speaks of accepting His world and His ways as your own. It declares Him Lord of your life, that you live for Him, and are committed to His Cause.

Jesus prayed to the Father saying:

"Your Kingdom come, Your will be done on earth as it is in heaven …"
[Matthew 6:10]

If that is our prayer – to introduce His world to our world – we should be taking it seriously. We aren't serving an archaic or dead God of a bygone era. He is alive and changing our world today. We may live *in* this world, but we aren't *of* this world. It is when we encounter Jesus that our world collides with His world and changes us forever. Our salvation is not found in the world we live in, nor are the answers to life. While our feet may be firmly planted in this world, our hope is found in His world.

Is He your world?

Can you say to the Lord, "You are my world?" For many Christians, it is probably more honest to say, "You are *in* my world." There are those who come to church to worship Him, instead of embracing a lifestyle of worship, allowing God only a *part of* their world.

Then there are others who have the safe-haven approach to Christianity, crying to God, "Take me out of this world." Sadly, they are missing the point. Some Christians think that God is against this world, but the Bible clearly says, "God so loved the world that He gave His only begotten Son" (John 3:16). He has given His best because He loves it so much. Rather than packing their bags and preparing to leave, Christians must focus on living effective lives in this world with the emphasis on others.

Finally, there are those who seem to be caught between two worlds, having one foot in each camp. Jesus distinctly said that you cannot serve two masters. To say "You are my world" reveals certain choices have been made: the choice about who you worship, where you invest and who you represent.

Jesus said:

"Where your *treasure* is, there your *heart* will be also." [Matthew 6:21]

When He is your world, you will treasure what He treasures, love what He loves and your heart will be committed to His Cause. There are three things that

God treasures: firstly, He loves His Son, Jesus; secondly, He loves lost people; and thirdly, He loves His bride – His Church. By making these three things your highest priorities, you begin to be effective for the Cause.

When Jesus faced the accusations of Pilate, He put His world and this world in perspective:

"Jesus answered, "My kingdom is not of this world. If My kingdom were of this world, My servants would fight, so that I should not be delivered to the Jews; but now My kingdom is not from here." [John 18:36]

He then went on to speak of His purpose,

"*For this cause* I was born, and *for this cause* I have come into the world."
[John 18:37]

We have been allotted a certain span of time on this earth, and we have one shot at life. To know the Cause is to understand why you were **born**, to know what you are **alive** for, and to recognise what you will **die** for. It is all about Christ and His Cause.

"THE CAUSE ..."

It is all about living beyond ourselves and bringing His world to our world.

It is about laying down our vision and recognising that we are born for a powerful Cause.

It is about making choices that ultimately put the Kingdom first in our everyday lives.

It is about building partnerships and relationships that *together* have greater impact in fulfilling the Cause.

It is about rejecting the middle ground, living a life of passion and conviction where He is always our first priority.

It is about dying to *self* and allowing 'Christ in *you*' to have pre-eminence in your life.

It is essentially about *building His Church*, with a revelation of eternity that goes well beyond us.

And ultimately, it is an honour and a privilege to know that we have been born for, can live for and die for the One who has done it all for us.

I pray this book has given you a perspective on your past, a motivation for today and a hope for the future, and that you too will be determined to discover the power of the Cause in your life.

FOR THIS CAUSE ...

ALSO AVAILABLE FROM MAXIMISED LEADERSHIP INC.

❝ One day during worship I asked the Lord to show me His heartbeat concerning His Church. I sensed the Spirit of God respond to my request with this precise answer, "Bobbie, when I look at my beautiful people, I call them three things. I call them a Family, a Body and a House."

Then I felt the Spirit say, "When I call them a Family, it is about unconditional love and acceptance. When I call them a Body, it is about effective function; and when I call them a House, it is about seriously reaching the world."

I then felt the Holy Spirit say, "Teach it." ❞ — Bobbie Houston

---

For further information on other books and resource material by Brian &
Bobbie Houston, write to:
Maximised Leadership Inc.
PO Box 1195, Castle Hill NSW 1765 Australia
www.maximisedleadership.com